This Awareness of Beauty

This Awareness of Beauty

THE ORCHESTRAL AND WIND BAND MUSIC OF HEALEY WILLAN

Keith W. Kinder

WILFRID LAURIER UNIVERSITY PRESS

Wilfrid Laurier University Press acknowledges the support of the Canada Council for the Arts for our publishing program. We acknowledge the financial support of the Government of Canada through the Canada Book Fund for our publishing activities.

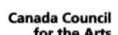

Library and Archives Canada Cataloguing in Publication

Kinder, Keith, author
    This awareness of beauty : the orchestral and wind band music of Healey Willan / Keith William Kinder.

Includes bibliographical references and index.
Issued in print and electronic formats.
ISBN 978-1-55458-960-9 (cloth).—ISBN 978-1-77112-127-9 (paper).—
ISBN 978-1-55458-962-3 (epub).—ISBN 978-1-55458-961-6 (pdf)

    1. Willan, Healey, 1880–1968—Criticism and interpretation. 2. Willan, Healey, 1880–1968. Orchestra music. 3. Willan, Healey, 1880–1968. Band music. I. Title.

MT92.W689K52 2014   784.2092   C2014-900205-X
                                            C2014-900206-8

Cover design by Sandra Friesen. Front-cover image of Healey Willan © Canada Post Corporation (1980). Text design by James Leahy.

© 2014 Wilfrid Laurier University Press
Waterloo, Ontario, Canada
www.wlupress.wlu.ca

This book is printed on FSC recycled paper and is certified Ecologo. It is made from 100% post-consumer fibre, processed chlorine free, and manufactured using biogas energy.

Printed in Canada

Every reasonable effort has been made to acquire permission for copyright material used in this text, and to acknowledge all such indebtedness accurately. Any errors and omissions called to the publisher's attention will be corrected in future printings.

No part of this publication may be reproduced, stored in a retrieval system, or transmitted, in any form or by any means, without the prior written consent of the publisher or a licence from the Canadian Copyright Licensing Agency (Access Copyright). For an Access Copyright licence, visit http://www.accesscopyright.ca or call toll free to 1-800-893-5777.

*This awareness of beauty,
the sudden recognition that one has somehow enlarged,
that one's spirit has soared,
is perhaps what the word inspiration attempts to convey.*

Healey Willan, 1958

Contents

List of Musical Examples ix
Preface and Acknowledgements xv

"English by Birth, Irish by Extraction, Canadian by Adoption, and Scotch by Absorption": Introduction and Biographical Sketch   1

Part One: *"Tender, Lyrical, Forceful, Arresting"*:
The Orchestral Music   19

1 Early Orchestral Works   23
2 Works for Small Orchestra   39
3 Shorter Orchestral Works   47
4 Works for Piano and Orchestra   73
5 The Symphonies   93

Part Two: *"A Couple of Very Pretty Tunes"*:
Works for Wind Band   137

6 Concert Band Works   139
7 Pedagogical Music   163
8 The Fanfares   169
Conclusion   181

Appendix: Works Reviewed with Sources   183
Notes   185
Bibliography   211
Index   215

Musical Examples

1.1 *[Allegro Marcato]*, bars 1–5 / 24
1.2 *Epilogue*, bars 1–4 / 26
1.3 *Epilogue*, bars 39–52 / 26
1.4 *Epilogue*, bars 81–88 / 27
1.5 *Epilogue*, bars 137–54 / 27
1.6 *Epilogue*, bars 212–16 / 28
1.7 *Through Darkness into Light*, bars 1–2 / 30
1.8 *Through Darkness into Light*, bars 22–23 / 30
1.9 *Through Darkness into Light*, bars 28–51 / 31
1.10 *Through Darkness into Light*, bars 53–54 (A1) / 31
1.11 *Through Darkness into Light*, bars 105–8 (B1) / 32
1.12 *Through Darkness into Light*, bars 116–17 / 32
1.13 *Through Darkness into Light*, bars 164–67 / 32
1.14 *Through Darkness into Light*, bars 250–60 / 33
1.15 *[Lento mistico]*, bars 13–20 (horn solo) / 35
1.16 *[Lento mistico]*, bars 35–38 / 35
1.17 *Rhapsody "From the Highlands,"* bars 69–71 / 37
1.18 Overture, bars 20–22 / 37
2.1 Overture to *The Alchemist*, bars 1–9 / 40
2.2 Overture to *The Alchemist*, bars 10–14 / 41
2.3 Overture to *The Alchemist*, bars 24–39 / 41
2.4 Overture to *The Alchemist*, bars 40–48 / 42
2.5 Overture to *The Alchemist*, bars 59–67 / 43
2.6 *Overture to an Unwritten Comedy*, bars 12–19 / 44
2.7 *Overture to an Unwritten Comedy*, bars 28–31 / 44
2.8 *Overture to an Unwritten Comedy*, bars 32–39 / 45

2.9   *Overture to an Unwritten Comedy,* bars 50–53 / 45
2.10 *Overture to an Unwritten Comedy,* bars 112–14 / 46
3.1   *Coronation March,* bars 3–12 / 49
3.2   *Coronation March,* bars 31–39 / 50
3.3   *Coronation March,* bars 51–59 / 51
3.4   *Coronation March,* bars 87–115 / 52–54
3.5   *A Marching Tune,* bars 3–18 / 56
3.6   *A Marching Tune,* bars 45–69 / 57
3.7   *Fugue in G Minor,* bars 1–4 / 59
3.8   *Royal Salute,* bars 6–13 / 60
3.9   *Royal Salute,* bars 76–88 / 61
3.10 *Poem,* bars 1–20 / 63
3.11 *Poem,* bars 44–60 / 64
3.12 *Poem,* bars 68–76 / 64
3.13 *Centennial (Ceremonial) March,* bars 13–23 (theme one) / 66
3.14 *Centennial (Ceremonial) March,* bars 37–38 / 67
3.15 *Centennial (Ceremonial) March,* bars 47–58 (theme two) / 67
3.16 *Centennial (Ceremonial) March,* bars 74–93 (ceremonial theme) / 68
3.17 *Largo,* bars 1–2 / 69
3.18 *Largo,* bars 7–26 / 70
4.1   *Ballade,* bars 1–2 / 74
4.2   *Ballade,* bars 16–20 / 74
4.3   *Ballade,* bars 28–31 / 75
4.4   *Ballade,* bars 35–42 / 75
4.5   *Ballade,* bars 104–11 / 76
4.6   *Ballade,* bars 186–99 / 76
4.7   *Ballade,* bars 219–22 / 76
4.8   Piano Concerto in C Minor, bars 3–9 (P1) / 79
4.9   Piano Concerto in C Minor, bars 21–23 (P2) / 79
4.10 Piano Concerto in C Minor, 55–61 (P3) / 80
4.11 Piano Concerto in C Minor, bars 70–72 (P4) / 80
4.12 Piano Concerto in C Minor, bars 101–5 (S1) / 81
4.13 Piano Concerto in C Minor, bars 140–43 ("Willan motto") / 81
4.14 Piano Concerto in C Minor, bar 173–81 / 82
4.15 Piano Concerto in C Minor, bars 270–74 / 82
4.16 Piano Concerto in C Minor, bars 280–93 / 83
4.17 Piano Concerto in C Minor, bars 312–14 / 83

4.18	Piano Concerto in C Minor, bars 333–35 / 84	
4.19	Piano Concerto in C Minor, bars 345–46 / 85	
4.20	Piano Concerto in C Minor, bars 362–70 / 86	
4.21	Piano Concerto in C Minor, bars 387–402 (1P) / 87	
4.22	Piano Concerto in C Minor, bars 438–42 (1S) / 87	
4.23	Piano Concerto in C Minor, bars 442–43 (2S) / 88	
4.24	Piano Concerto in C Minor, bars 449–57 (3S) / 88	
4.25	Piano Concerto in C Minor, bars 565–69 / 89	
4.26	Piano Concerto in C Minor, bars 616–22 / 90	
5.1	Symphony No. 1, first movement, bars 2–5 (I1) / 94	
5.2	Symphony No. 1, first movement, bar 7 / 95	
5.3	Symphony No. 1, first movement, bars 26–30 / 95	
5.4	Symphony No. 1, first movement, bars 31–34 (P1) / 96	
5.5	Symphony No. 1, first movement, bars 54–55 / 96	
5.6	Symphony No. 1, first movement, bars 66–67 (P2—winds) / 96	
5.7	Symphony No. 1, first movement, bars 138–47 (S1) / 97	
5.8	Symphony No. 1, first movement, bars 171–74 (S2) / 98	
5.9	Symphony No. 1, first movement, bars 212–19 / 99	
5.10	Symphony No. 1, first movement, bars 246–48 / 99	
5.11	Symphony No. 1, second movement, bars 1–2 (motive 1) / 101	
5.12	Symphony No. 1, second movement, bars 6–10 (motive 2) / 101	
5.13	Symphony No. 1, second movement, bars 11–15 (theme one) / 101	
5.14	Symphony No. 1, second movement, bars 17–20 (solo oboe) / 101	
5.15	Symphony No. 1, second movement, bars 29–30 (theme two—flute solo) / 102	
5.16	Symphony No. 1, second movement, bars 36–41 (theme three) / 102	
5.17	Symphony No. 1, third movement, bar 4 (1M) / 104	
5.18	Symphony No. 1, third movement, bars 6–7 (2M) / 104	
5.19	Symphony No. 1, third movement, bars 4–8 (1P) / 105	
5.20	Symphony No. 1, third movement, bars 11–14 (2P) / 105	
5.21	Symphony No. 1, third movement, bars 36–38 (3P) / 105	
5.22	Symphony No. 1, third movement, bars 57–58 (bars 54–55 of *Lento mistico*) / 106	
5.23	Symphony No. 1, third movement, bars 60–73 (S) / 107	

5.24 Symphony No. 1, third movement, bars 112–17 / 107
5.25 Symphony No. 1, third movement, bars 295–301 / 108
5.26 Symphony No. 1, third movement, bars 345–50 (brass parts only) / 110
5.27 Symphony No. 2, first movement, bars 1–3 / 112
5.28 Symphony No. 2, first movement, bars 2–8 (I1) / 112
5.29 Symphony No. 2, first movement, bars 30–32 / 113
5.30 Symphony No. 2, first movement, bars 34–39 / 113
5.31 Symphony No. 2, first movement, bars 40–48 (P1) / 114
5.32 Symphony No. 2, first movement, bars 50–56 (P2) / 114
5.33 Symphony No. 2, first movement, bar 60 / 114
5.34 Symphony No. 2, first movement, bars 71–76 (P3) / 115
5.35 Symphony No. 2, first movement, bars 79–80 (horn call) / 115
5.36 Symphony No. 2, first movement, bars 85–86 / 115
5.37 Symphony No. 2, first movement, bars 93–100 (P4) / 115
5.38 Symphony No. 2, first movement, bars 111–13 (S1) / 116
5.39 Symphony No. 2, first movement, bars 116–24 / 116
5.40 Symphony No. 2, first movement, bars 146–52 / 117
5.41 Symphony No. 2, first movement, bars 156–59 (trumpets) / 117
5.42 Symphony No. 2, first movement, bars 160–65 (oboe) / 118
5.43 Symphony No. 2, first movement, bars 169–91 (Development theme) / 118
5.44 Symphony No. 2, first movement, bars 219–25 (subject and counter-subject) / 119
5.45 Symphony No. 2, first movement, bars 315–17 (horns and trumpets) / 120
5.46 Symphony No. 2, first movement, bars 321–22 / 121
5.47 Symphony No. 2, second movement, bars 5–22 (theme one) / 122
5.48 Symphony No. 2, second movement, bars 42–50 / 122
5.49 Symphony No. 2, second movement, bars 50–60 (theme two and development, solo lines only) / 123
5.50 Symphony No. 2, second movement, bars 101–8 / 124
5.51 Symphony No. 2, second movement, bars 110–13 (horn) / 124
5.52 Symphony No. 2, third movement, bars 2–16 (theme one—subject and answer) / 126

5.53 Symphony No. 2, third movement, bars 34–42 (theme two) / 127
5.54 Symphony No. 2, third movement, bars 42–46 / 127
5.55 Symphony No. 2, third movement, bars 59–62 (strings) / 128
5.56 Symphony No. 2, third movement, bars 63–67 (horns—theme three) / 128
5.57 Symphony No. 2, third movement, bars 104–7 (oboe—theme four) / 128
5.58 Symphony No. 2, third movement, bars 168–71 (oboe) / 129
5.59 Symphony No. 2, third movement, bars 188–91 / 129
5.60 Symphony No. 2, third movement, bars 250–57 / 130
5.61 Symphony No. 2, third movement, bars 302–8 / 130
5.62 Symphony No. 2, fourth movement, bars 10–16 (1I) / 132
5.63 Symphony No. 2, fourth movement, bars 15–17 / 132
5.64 Symphony No. 2, fourth movement, bars 28–38 (1P) / 133
5.65 Symphony No. 2, fourth movement, bars 49–53 (2P—horns) / 133
5.66 Symphony No. 2, fourth movement, bars 89–92 / 133
5.67 Symphony No. 2, fourth movement, bars 93–97 / 134
5.68 Symphony No. 2, fourth movement, bars 101–12 (1S) / 134
5.69 Symphony No. 2, fourth movement, bars 190–93 / 135
6.1 *Royce Hall Suite*—Prelude and Fugue, bars 1–3 / 145
6.2 *Royce Hall Suite*—Prelude and Fugue, bar 10 / 145
6.3 *Royce Hall Suite*—Prelude and Fugue, bars 16–18 (fugue subject and counter-subject) / 146
6.4 *Royce Hall Suite*—Prelude and Fugue, bars 55–56 (*stretto* effect) / 146
6.5 *Royce Hall Suite*—Prelude and Fugue, bars 65–68 / 147
6.6 *Royce Hall Suite*—Menuet, bars 30–32 / 148
6.7 *Royce Hall Suite*—Menuet, bars 5–7 / 148
6.8 *Royce Hall Suite*—Menuet, bars 26–29 / 148
6.9 *Royce Hall Suite*—Rondo, bars 1–11 (main theme) / 149
6.10 *Royce Hall Suite*—Rondo, bars 23–32 / 150
6.11 *Royce Hall Suite*—Rondo, bars 78–85 / 150
6.12 *Royce Hall Suite*—Rondo, bars 126–33 / 151
6.13 *Élégie héroïque*, bars 1–7 (fanfare) / 155

6.14 *Élégie héroïque*, bars 11–20 (theme one) / 155
6.15 *Élégie héroïque*, bars 20–45 (theme two) / 156
6.16 *Élégie héroïque*, bars 56–64 (melody and countermelody) / 156
6.17 *Ceremonial March for the Canadian Centennial*, bars 13–23 (theme one) / 159
6.18 *Ceremonial March for the Canadian Centennial*, bars 37–38 / 160
6.19 *Ceremonial March for the Canadian Centennial*, bars 47–58 (theme two) / 160
6.20 *Ceremonial March for the Canadian Centennial*, bars 74–93 (Ceremonial theme) / 161
7.1 *Suite for Rhythm Band*—March, bars 13–20 (first strain) / 164
7.2 *Suite for Rhythm Band*—March, bars 45–52 (second strain) / 164
7.3 *Suite for Rhythm Band*—March, bars 71–79 (third strain) / 164
7.4 *Suite for Rhythm Band*—Intermezzo, bars 3–13 (A section melody) / 165
7.5 *Suite for Rhythm Band*—Intermezzo, bars 34–49 (B section melody) / 165
7.6 *Suite for Rhythm Band*—Jig, bars 1–4 (subject and counter-subject) / 166
7.7 *Suite for Rhythm Band*—Jig, bars 16–17 (subject inverted) / 000
8.1 "Flourish," bars 1–5 / 171
8.2 *Ceremonial Fanfare No. 2*, bars 8–9 / 175
8.3 *Ceremonial Fanfare No. 3*, bars 16–20 / 175
8.4 *Fanfare No. 1*, bars 7–8 / 177
8.5 *No. 3 (or 1)*, bars 1–5 / 177

Preface and Acknowledgements

Researching and writing about Canadian musicians often involve complications and opportunities that may not arise when working in other areas. Musicological inquiry on Canadian topics is still a rather young endeavour. The published resource materials on many (perhaps most) individuals is incomplete, leaving researchers to explore primary sources such as personal contacts and limited media reports in order to fill in items such as biographical and other personal details. Recording the circumstances attending the creation of specific compositions is more complicated and often can only be documented through performers' reminiscences or by word of mouth. While the limitations of resource materials offer challenges to Canadian researchers, they also provide a wide range of possible areas of inquiry and the potential for intriguing new discoveries.

In Canadian musicological research, Healey Willan is something of an exception. His importance to Canadian music as composer, teacher, performer, and conductor was recognized quickly after his arrival in Canada in 1913 and has been thoroughly documented. Writing about Willan's music, however, has focused on his choral and organ compositions—the works upon which his enduring international reputation is based and those that are, probably quite rightly, seen as his most important creations. His instrumental music has attracted considerably less scholarly investigation, and, until this study, no one has subjected his wind band output to any kind of historical/musical/critical evaluation, despite its seminal place in the history and development of Canadian wind band repertoire.

However, this is not to say that Willan's orchestral music has been ignored by researchers, even though their focus has largely been elsewhere. Works like his Symphony No. 2 and the Piano Concerto in C Minor have many admirers, and the little *Overture to an Unwritten Comedy* appears frequently on Canadian orchestral programs. This study, however, incorporates all of this composer's extant orchestral music with the intention of broadening our understanding of the celebrated works, bringing the lesser-known compositions more directly into the consciousness of scholars and conductors, and correcting some errors that have crept into the literature.

For researchers interested in Canadian wind band music, the existing resources are sparse, indeed. Wind music researchers face an often daunting task of piecing together an understanding of the historical background of this repertoire from oblique references in the resource material, from interviews with the composer him or herself (if possible), with family and associates such as conductors, and perhaps from a few scattered mentions in the print or other media. Like explorations of any other repertoire, musical/critical analyses are, of course, grounded in close readings of the primary sources—the scores themselves.

The relegation of wind band music to a secondary role in much Canadian music research is not difficult to understand. Rather little of this repertoire, written before the twenty-first century, was intended for professional performers or organizations. With the exception of the full-time military bands, most Canadian music in this genre is commissioned and performed by ensembles in secondary and post-secondary educational institutions. Both researchers and composers often see such music as "utilitarian" and unworthy of their best efforts. To combat this conception, initiatives such as the Canadian Music Centre's John Adaskin Project have over many years encouraged Canada's leading composers to produce works specifically for educationally based performers, and many of the pieces generated under these auspices are of fine quality.[1]

By contrast, in the United States, the commitment of university-based wind conductors to new music and a universally impressive performance standard, especially among university, college, and top-level military wind bands, have generated considerable enthusiasm for the wind band medium among prominent composers who continue to create a substantial, innovative repertoire at the highest standards of musical/aesthetic content.[2] In Canada, only about fifteen universities maintain the comprehensive music programs (with graduate performance majors on wind instruments) that exist at virtually every state and many privately funded American universities, with the result that the demand for Canadian repertoire at the higher levels of difficulty is substantially reduced. However, works commissioned by wind ensembles at the Canadian universities with the most comprehensive music programs are every bit as musically sophisticated and challenging as those produced in the United States.

In comparison with his productivity in other genres, Willan's orchestral and wind band music comprises a small part of his total output. Nevertheless, this composer's central role in Canadian music in the twentieth century virtually demands that this music be seriously investigated, a demand that is thoroughly justified by its high quality.

No project of this scope is possible without the assistance of many individuals and institutions. I would especially like to thank Maureen Nevins, Florence Hayes, Bronwen Masemann, and all of the staff of the Music Division of Library and Archives Canada in Ottawa for their prompt, thorough, and informative responses to requests for materials, their willingness to dig out answers to unusual questions, and for facilitating visits to explore the enormous Willan archive. Bronwen Quarry of the Hudson's Bay Archives in Winnipeg provided a wealth of informative detail about the curious ceremony in 1959 that produced two outstanding brass fanfares by Willan, reviewed later in this study. The staff at the Canadian Music Centre, Toronto, willingly sought out unusual or missing scores. I am greatly indebted to Master Warrant Officer David A. Druce, the Band Sergeant Major of the Ceremonial Guard in Ottawa, who provided contact information for Captain Charles Adams (CD, LRAM, ARCM). My communications with Captain Adams resulted in not only information about Willan's *Ceremonial March for the Canadian Centennial* and Adams's outstanding band transcription of it, but also a completed full score and parts to the transcription, as well as the opportunity to schedule the second performance of this march at McMaster University. Performance materials for this work are now preserved in the National Library of Canada, Ottawa, and the Canadian Music Centre, Toronto. Captain Adams deserves the appreciation of band conductors everywhere for making this admirable composition available to us. I encourage the performance of this march regularly in order that we may sometime soon see its commercial publication. Graham Coles and Mary Plumley at Berandol Music, and officials at Concordia Publishing House, C.F. Peters Corporation, European American Music provided scores and parts that immeasurably assisted my analytical work on these compositions.

And, last, but by no means least, my deepest appreciation to my wife, Susan Smith, for her ceaseless encouragement, support, and love.

"*English by Birth, Irish by Extraction, Canadian by Adoption, and Scotch by Absorption*":
Introduction and Biographical Sketch

Healey Willan is widely regarded as the "Dean of English Canadian composers" (Clarke 1983, x). He earned that title through his nearly forty-year association with the University of Toronto and the Toronto Conservatory,[1] during which time he taught virtually an entire generation of English-speaking Canadian musicians. Willan is one of a very few Canadian composers who have achieved lasting international reputations. His exquisite choral and masterful organ music is performed by choirs and organists the world over. While these works are deservedly famous, Willan's compositions encompassed a wide variety of genres, including those of the orchestra and the wind band that are the focus of this study.

The specifics of Willan's life have been admirably explicated by F.R.C. Clarke,[2] Thomas C. Brown,[3] and Giles Bryant,[4] and need not be revisited in detail here. However, a brief biography has been provided to illustrate the origins and development of Willan's compositional style and establish a context for the works that will be addressed below. Most of the biographical, and much of the analytical, information offered is drawn from Clarke's seminal book, *Healey Willan: Life and Music* (see Bibliography), and readers who desire a more thorough understanding of Willan's biography are referred to Clarke.

England

James Healey Willan was born on October 12, 1880, in Balham, Surrey, England. His family was not especially musical, although his mother, Eleanor (Healey) Willan,[5] was an amateur pianist who also played organ in church services. She was his first music teacher. In 1882 the family moved to Beckenham in Kent, and Healey's first parochial experiences were at the Church of St. George, which followed the "high Anglican" (or Anglo-Catholic) rite.[6] Willan was fascinated by the sound of plainchant from an early age, a fascination that, as will be seen, had a profound effect that survived throughout his career.[7]

In later life, Willan was to claim that he was born with an innate ability to read music, and whether or not this was true, he certainly displayed prodigious talent while still very young. His piano instruction began at age five, but he had discovered the basic chords on the keyboard well before he understood them in technical terms. When he was nine years old, his family relocated to Eastbourne in Sussex, and Willan was admitted to a choir school associated with St. Saviour's Church. Apparently his initial entry into the school felt like he "was going to his execution" (Clarke 1983, 5), but within a year he had written and performed his first composition, a March in A (no longer extant) for piano.[8] By age eleven he was playing organ for some of the evensongs and directing choral rehearsals, although this brought him into conflict with some of the older boys and the master had to intervene to protect him from their physical attacks. When he left the school at age fifteen he had a secure background in many subjects but had decided that music would be his profession. Over the next year, while recovering from illness, he indulged in a rigorous program of self-study in harmony and counterpoint, after which he was able to declare: "Writing counterpoint lost its terrors for me, and I have always enjoyed it" (Clarke 1983, 7). Contrapuntal skills acquired during that year sustained Willan throughout his career, and he constantly encouraged his own students to engage in similar intensive studies.[9]

In the mid-1890s, Willan's family moved to the cathedral town of St. Albans in Hertfordshire, not far from London. Willan began intensive organ studies with Dr. William Stevenson Hoyte, a highly respected teacher and organist at All Saints', Margaret Street, London.[10] He studied piano with an equally celebrated teacher, Evlyn Howard-Jones.[11] As a result of the instruction he received from these teachers, he passed the examinations to become a Fellow of the Royal College of Organists at eighteen years of age—the youngest candidate ever to be awarded the diploma. On presenting the diploma to the young man, Sir Hubert Parry wondered if Willan was actually accepting it on behalf of his father! (Clarke 1983, 8).

Willan also began his professional career in St. Albans. In January 1898, he became the organist at the small church of St. Saviour's in St. Albans, where he formed a women's choir, the St Cecilia Choir, which promptly became an important part of the musical life of the church. In the same year his eucharistic hymn *All Hail! All Hail!* became his first published composition. His *Sanctus, Benedictus and Agnus Dei in E-flat* for SSA and organ, written especially for the St. Cecilia Choir, was published two years later. Although still in his teens, Willan was already establishing himself as an important church musician and composer.

After two years, he left St. Albans to assume a better position at Christ Church, Wanstead, in northeast London. This church had substantial resources, and he began presenting large-scale choral/orchestral compositions such as Mendelssohn's *Lobegesang* and *St. Paul*. In addition to his duties as organist and choir director, he gave organ recitals and taught lessons in harmony, counterpoint, organ, and piano. He also conducted the Wanstead Choral Society and a theatrical production of *The Pirates of Penzance*. This was the beginning of what would become his life's pattern. His musical activities were always centred on an important church position but included extensive efforts in the community as well. During the Wanstead years, he also became interested in orchestral music, travelling into London (often with some difficulty because of his limited financial means) to hear performances by that city's most prominent musical institutions. He also appeared for the only time as soloist with orchestra in Josef Rheinberger's Concerto No. 1 in F for organ and orchestra (Clarke 1983, 9–10). While orchestral music as a compositional medium interested him throughout his career, and he completed three works and sketched at least three others prior to 1911, he composed few significant orchestral works before the 1930s.

In mid-1903 Willan assumed the position of organist/choirmaster at St. John the Baptist, Kensington, London, winning out over some 130 candidates for the post. He thoroughly enjoyed this appointment and held it for the rest of his time in England. Not surprisingly, St. John the Baptist was Anglo-Catholic and considered to be a prestigious position.[12] Since Willan had been thoroughly immersed in the Anglo-Catholic doctrine[13] from an early age, he felt very comfortable at St. John the Baptist and gradually developed a reputation as an authority on vernacular plainsong (in English rather than Latin). As with his earlier position, he worked extensively outside his church. He continued to teach and became the conductor of the local theatrical group, the Thalian Operatic Society, which specialized in Gilbert and Sullivan operettas. He accepted positions as organist for two organizations, the Guild of All Souls and the English Church Union, which presented large-scale choral festivals once or twice a year. He was often also responsible for training the choirs for these events.

Throughout his London years, other influences were to have a significant impact on his future. Sir Richard Terry,[14] director of music at Westminster Cathedral, frequently performed Renaissance polyphonic music in his services, a rarity at the time. Willan heard works by Palestrina, Victoria, and composers of the English Renaissance under Terry's direction. He also made the acquaintance of Francis Burgess, musical director of the London Gregorian Association, and a proponent of the revival of plainsong and its re-establishment in churches. Willan joined the association in 1910 and participated in its annual Gregorian festivals at St. Paul's Cathedral, which often involved hundreds of singers. He contributed a fauxbourdon[15] for the processional hymn in the 1912 festival, which was praised as "worthy of the best 16th-century traditions" (Clarke 1983, 13). These experiences undoubtedly influenced him, many years later, to form his own Tudor Singers in Toronto, specifically to perform this same repertoire.

His life changed in other ways as well. On November 29, 1905, he married a well-trained musician, Gladys Ellen Hall, a pianist and singer who had studied at the Royal Academy of Music.[16] Together they raised four children and would remain married for nearly sixty years.

He also continued to compose. By 1908, he had a number of important publications of choral music, songs, organ music, and the Romance in E-flat for violin and piano. By 1913, he had written more than seventy songs, a number of organ works, choral music, three symphonic compositions, sketched a number of other orchestral pieces, and produced some chamber music. Enough of his music had been published that he attracted the attention of prominent musicians who saw him as a promising young composer. One of his choral works, *Ave verum corpus*, published in 1909, was to have an unexpected impact on his future. The work became known in Canada, and when the position of head of the theory department at the Toronto Conservatory became vacant, Willan was identified as a candidate for the opening. He accepted the posting in March 1913 and arrived in Toronto in late August.

Willan's decision to emigrate was at least partly motivated by financial considerations. Despite his busy life and multiple positions in London, his budgetary situation was always insecure.[17] By 1913 he had a wife and three sons, and early that year his father had died, leaving him responsible for his mother and sister as well. The appointment at the Toronto Conservatory offered a substantial increase in salary and the promise of a comfortable life (Clarke 1983, 3–16). Besides, Willan believed that the numbers 3 and 13 played an important part in his life. The offer from the Toronto Conservatory had arrived on the third day of the third month in 1913, when he was 33! How could he not accept the position (Brown and Bryant 1992, 1405)?

Canada

After arriving in Toronto, Willan quickly immersed himself in the musical life of the city. Three weeks (another 3!) after his arrival he was appointed organist and choir director at St. Paul's Church, Bloor Street. A huge new building was nearing completion, which would house a purpose-built organ that would be among the largest in North America. At the official opening of the building in November, Willan's Te Deum in B-flat (1906) was sung. The organ was not completed for several months, but for its dedication on April 29, 1914, he composed what is generally considered to be his masterwork for organ, the Introduction, Passacaglia and Fugue in E-flat Minor. This instrument also inspired him to give an extensive series of recitals—nearly thirty at St. Paul's between 1914 and 1917. This accomplishment represented a substantial contribution to the musical activity in the city. After 1917, his recital activity moved to other locations in Toronto, as well as the surrounding region. Many of these involved the dedication of a new organ (Clarke 1983, 17).

However, despite a salary more than four times what he had made at St. John the Baptist, and the availability of the finest organ ever to be at his disposal, he was not content at St. Paul's. The church followed the "low Anglican" tradition, which did not suit his background and interests. He remained at St. Paul's until 1921, then gave himself a birthday present by resigning on October 12.[18]

Willan was active in other musical spheres as well. In 1914, he became an examiner for the Faculty of Music at the University of Toronto, beginning an association that would last until 1950. He joined the Arts and Letters Club in 1915, where he was able to consort with artists of all callings and engage in stimulating conversation (Clarke 1983, 18).[19]

In the meantime his reputation as a composer was growing. A complete concert of his works was given in Toronto in April 1916, another in Montreal in February 1926, at the Church of St. Andrew and St. Paul.[20] Three of his most important chamber works, Trio in B-flat Minor (violin, cello, and piano), Sonata in E Minor (violin and piano), and *Variations and Epilogue on an Original Theme* (two pianos), were completed within a few years of his arrival in Toronto. The Trio and the Sonata were performed at this time,[21] but the *Variations and Epilogue* had to wait until 1941 to be heard. He also composed a number of sacred works that were performed in prominent situations. These included the eight-part a capella motet *The Dead* for the Toronto Mendelssohn Choir, commemorating members killed in the First World War, and the anthem *In the Name of God We Will Set Up Our Banners* for the depositing of military colours in St. Paul's. As a performer, he travelled to other parts of Canada and to the United States (Clarke 1983, 19).

The 1920s were a particularly important time both personally and professionally. In 1920 the University of Toronto awarded him the first of several honorary doctorates that he would receive (Beckwith 1997, 143). The same year he purchased a house at 139 Inglewood Drive in Toronto (the address includes many combinations of 3 and 13!) to accommodate his family, which now included a daughter, Mary, as well as his three sons. He was promoted to vice-principal of the

From the point of view of this study, two events from 1949 require special mention. In May, Willan provided a fanfare and fauxbourdons for the enthronement of the archbishop in St. George's Cathedral, Kingston, Ontario. The fanfare (in reality a "flourish") was scored for four trumpets and will be addressed in detail later in this study. More important was his engagement as visiting professor (teaching courses in choir and church music) at the University of California, Los Angeles, during the summers of 1948 and 1949. This engagement led to his being commissioned to compose his most important wind band work, *Royce Hall Suite* (Clarke 1983, 42–43).

Although Willan always engaged in a plethora of musical enterprises, his schedule during the 1940s was extremely demanding. While he was composing these large-scale works, he was also teaching, directing his church choir, performing outside Toronto, and engaging in charitable activities. While he clearly enjoyed being busy, this intense activity damaged his health. In February 1947, he suffered a heart attack and was forced to convalesce until the end of May. Fortunately, he made an almost complete recovery and by the summer was back at most of his earlier activities.

Retirement

At the end of June 1950, Willan retired from the University of Toronto. However, his withdrawal from teaching did not translate into reduced activities in other areas. He had always been concerned with elevating the quality of music performed in the church, and when several publishers (including Concordia Publishing House, Oxford University Press, and C.F. Peters) asked him to add to their catalogues of sacred music, he felt obligated to respond. He composed and published an enormous quantity of short liturgical pieces, at many levels of difficulty, not always with the most memorable musical results. He also received a number of commissions intended to mark important anniversaries, and these longer works include some of his finest efforts.[40]

His seventieth birthday on October 12, 1950, was marked by a number of commemorative events. Concerts of his music were given in St. Paul's, Bloor Street, before an audience of more than 2,000, and on the CBC. As noted earlier, the Toronto Symphony under MacMillan gave two performances (November 7 and 8) of the Symphony No. 2. Several composers wrote celebratory works.[41]

Willan was always proud of his British roots, and during the early 1950s he was feted on several occasions in his native land. On Dominion Day (July 1), 1951, the BBC broadcast the recording of the Piano Concerto and subsequently asked Willan and the St. Mary Magdalene Singers to prepare a special program to be broadcast on November 22 (St. Cecilia's Day) over its international service. Also in 1951, he composed what has become his most popular orchestral work, the short *Overture to an Unwritten Comedy*. This bright, energetic piece was first heard on a CBC broadcast with John Adaskin[42] conducting the CBC Toronto Orchestra (Bryant 1972, 43) and has become a favourite of Canadian conductors.

The following year, the royal concert given in the Royal Festival Hall, London, on St. Cecilia's Day, included *An Apostrophe to the Heavenly Hosts*. Through the generosity of the congregation at St. Mary Magdalene, Willan was able to attend and was presented to Queen Elizabeth. The performance was excellent, and the *Times* called the work "a surprise from Canada" (Clarke 1983, 49). As a direct result of this performance, Willan was asked to write a new work for the 1953 St. Cecilia's Day Festival,[43] and, more important, was invited to compose one of the homage anthems for the coronation of Queen Elizabeth II on June 2, 1953.[44] He was deeply honoured by this invitation—the only non-resident composer who was invited to participate. His anthem *O Lord, Our Governour* received a fine performance and was well received.

More recognition in England followed. In 1956 he was awarded a Lambeth Degree of Doctor of Music. Since this degree was bestowed by the Archbishop of Canterbury in recognition of outstanding service to the Anglican Church, it was highly prized by Willan. In December 1953, the BBC Orchestra and Chorus under Sir Adrian Boult[45] broadcast part of Willan's *Coronation Suite* to the Commonwealth, and in 1954 the BBC presented one of the rare performances of his *Variations and Epilogue on an Original Theme* for two pianos—a major work that still remains rarely performed.[46]

In Canada, he was becoming a cultural icon. In 1951, he received a National Award of Merit from the University of Alberta, Banff School of Fine Arts. Queen's University awarded him a Doctor of Letters in 1952 and the University of Manitoba followed suit in 1954. His birthday in 1955 was commemorated by a two-and-a-half-hour CBC national broadcast devoted to his life and music and by several special performances. As had occurred in 1950, St. Paul's hosted a concert of his music before a large audience. After the concert he was presented with an award of merit by the mayor of Toronto. He received numerous congratulatory letters and telegrams. In 1957, the Toronto Symphony was criticized for ignoring Willan's second symphony; an article in the *Toronto Daily Star* proposed that this work should replace yet another performance of the Tchaikovsky fifth symphony. The outpouring of public support for this view persuaded the *Star* to sponsor a special concert in March 1958. Walter Susskind[47] thoroughly prepared the score; the performance pleased Willan and was enthusiastically received. In 1959 the National Film Board of Canada made a short film, *Man of Music*, which ran as a "short" in commercial theatres for some time and introduced Willan to a large audience who otherwise would have had little opportunity to know anything about him or experience his music. Also in 1959, Queen Elizabeth II and Prince Philip visited Canada. Willan composed a *Royal Salute*, which was played by the CBC Symphony under Geoffrey Waddington, and, in July, when the Hudson's Bay Company presented a tribute to the queen in Winnipeg, he was commissioned to write two fanfares for the ceremony. Although he did not attend the event, the fanfares were well received. The Canadian Federation of Music Teachers Associations made him honorary president in 1959, and a year later the Royal Canadian College of Organists established a scholarship in his name (Clarke 1983, 49, 52–54, 56–58).

Age was also catching up to him. In 1957, he again experienced heart problems and was forced to curtail his activities at St. Mary Magdalene. He was also feeling the crippling effects of arthritis, and his doctor was concerned about cataracts. Despite these concerns, the National Film Board crew filming *Man of Music* was astonished by his energy, focus, and humour (Clarke 1983, 57).

Willan's eightieth birthday in 1960 drew letters of congratulation from all over North America and the British Isles. The Royal College of Organists in England sent official greetings and the *American Organist* printed an extensive tribute. The Toronto office of Oxford University Press hosted a birthday party that was attended by many prominent members of the musical world (Clarke 1983, 59).

The 1960s brought heartbreak and deteriorating health as well as continuing recognition and accomplishments. In December 1964, Willan's wife Gladys, his partner of nearly sixty years, died suddenly of a heart attack. He missed her terribly, and life at his home on Inglewood Drive became lonely. His daughter Mary heard him improvising at the piano the night after her mother died in what was apparently his elegy to his beloved wife. "It was very beautiful music," she reported (Clarke 1983, 62).

Early in the decade he experienced difficulties with both seeing and hearing, and lumbago forced the cancellation of a number of engagements. He was again hospitalized with a heart condition in the spring of 1963 and had bouts of influenza in 1963 and 1964. His eyesight, which had first been problematic in 1958, began to degenerate more quickly. He had an operation to remove cataracts in late 1967, and recovered very slowly. Prostate cancer was discovered in December, and family and friends prepared for the worst. He rallied, however, and returned home in February 1968 (Clarke 1983, 60–61, 66–67).

There were triumphs as well. In 1961 he was awarded the Canada Council Medal, and the following year he received an honorary Doctor of Laws from McMaster University. He was made a Fellow of the Royal School of Music in 1963, one of only a few "overseas" musicians so honoured. In December 1966, the CBC presented a television program, *Portrait of Healey Willan*, in which it had, with some difficulty, persuaded Willan to participate. During the Canadian centennial year, 1967, he was among the first recipients of the newly created Companion of the Order of Canada. Also in 1967, a special centennial concert of his chorus and organ works was presented before an audience of nearly 3,000 in St. Paul's. Willan received an enthusiastic standing ovation, which touched him deeply. The Canadian centennial apparently was of little interest to him,[48] but he did contribute a *Centennial Anthem*, which was performed on Parliament Hill in Ottawa on the eve of the centennial, December 31, 1966. His last orchestral composition, *Centennial March* or *Ceremonial March* (Willan apparently used both titles), was premiered in unusual circumstances in August at the Centennial Centre in Ottawa. These circumstances will be explored in detail later in this study (Clarke 1983, 59–60, 64–66).

In terms of composition, two projects preoccupied him during this time. In 1960, he had begun work on *The Canadian Psalter, Plainsong Edition*. An enormous undertaking, it absorbed him for three years but was a labour of love. He also worked intently on preparing his opera *Deidre* for stage performance. The work was produced twice: in 1965 the University of Toronto Opera School presented three performances in the MacMillan Theatre of the Faculty of Music, and the following year the Canadian Opera Company performed it at the O'Keefe Centre in Toronto—the first production of a Canadian opera by the COC (Bryant 1975, 240). Both productions were well received, much to the composer's satisfaction since he considered *Deidre* to be his masterpiece. A new version of *Brébeuf* was performed in September 1967. Willan conducted the choir (the last time he would conduct in public), and the performance was broadcast by the CBC to mark the feast of St. Jean de Brébeuf. A tribute to the composer followed the broadcast (Clarke 1983, 59, 62, 66).

With a supreme effort, he played the midnight mass at St. Mary Magdalene on Christmas Eve, 1967, but he was very weak and required a great deal of assistance. Healey Willan died quietly in his sleep at home on February 16, 1968 (Clarke 1983, 66–67).

Legacy

Willan's contribution to Canadian music was enormous and multi-faceted. When he arrived in Toronto in 1913, he immediately became a giant in the musical community. Few others resident in the city could boast a comparable comprehensive musical training, were as seasoned as performers, or were as experienced in directing choirs. While Willan did not claim to be an outstanding organist,[49] his numerous recitals at St. Paul's, at St. Mary Magdalene, and at the University of Toronto demonstrated what might be expected of a professional musician—the ability to perform often and in a variety of repertoire. His choirs at St. Mary Magdalene set a standard for choral performance that survived beyond his death in the work of other choral directors such as Elmer Iseler[50] (a former St. Mary Magdalene chorister) and Giles Bryant.

His teaching has also had a lasting influence. His long association with the University of Toronto's Faculty of Music allowed him to interact with virtually a complete generation of English-Canadian musicians. Willan had little interest in the musical developments of his time, which he dismissed as "strange sounds, which surprise and disturb me" (Brown and Bryant 1992, 1406). His credo was "to add to the beauty of the past, not to seek out the shape and sound of things to come" (Brown and Bryant 1992, 1406). Interestingly, he did not impose these views on his students. Godfrey Ridout[51] described his teaching as "engaging in a dialogue about works and suggesting improvements" (Brown and Bryant 1992, 1406). Louis Applebaum,[52] who distinguished himself as a film and theatre music composer (especially at the world-famous Stratford Shakespearean Festival in Stratford, Ontario), reported: "He had no truck with some of the newer things that were going on but that didn't matter … It never stood in the way of an association between you and him" (Brown and Bryant 1992, 1406). While he did not insist that his students follow his approach ("adding to the beauty of the past"), he did require a strong grounding in traditional harmony and counterpoint. One of his favourite expressions was: "He preachèd two-part counterpoint, but no one believèd him" (Clarke 1983, 79). Many of his students went on to thoroughly explore the mid-twentieth-century avant-garde.

From a compositional point of view, Willan's influence was no less profound. His musical education in England at the end of the nineteenth century was firmly based on the study of Bach, Handel, Mendelssohn, and the prominent British composers of the time, Hubert Parry, Charles Villiers Stanford, Arnold Bax, and Edward Elgar. He was also a great admirer of Brahms and Wagner. As he matured, he expressed admiration for Debussy, whose opera *Pelléas et Mélisande* influenced certain passages in *Deirdre of the Sorrows*. While Willan never abandoned the early-twentieth-century English style, within that framework he never ceased to evolve. Certain of Willan's compositions—*An Apostrophe to the Heavenly Hosts*; the liturgical motets; Introduction, Passacaglia and Fugue for organ—are universally recognized as masterpieces and hold established places in the international repertoire. Organists and choir directors admire the effectiveness and musical quality of a number of smaller works, which also have an international following.

Other works—Symphony No. 2, Piano Concerto in C Minor, Sonata in E Minor for violin and piano, the opera *Deirdre of the Sorrows*, *Royce Hall Suite* for concert band, *Variations and Epilogue on an Original Theme* for two pianos—are landmark compositions in Canadian music, holding very significant places in each genre. His place as the "Dean of English Canadian Composers" remains unchallenged.

PART ONE

"Tender, Lyrical, Forceful, Arresting": The Orchestral Music

Willan's early musical training does not appear to have included engagement with the orchestra or wind band. Instead, his study of piano, and especially organ, led him naturally to both sacred instrumental and choral music. His first published composition was a sacred choral work, the Eucharistic anthem *All Hail! All Hail!* which appeared in 1898 while he was still a teenager (Clarke 1983, 8). The art song was also an early interest, and some of the songs written in the 1890s illustrate aspects of his mature style.[1] His songs began to be published as early as 1901 (Clarke 1983, 204). Probably the experience of writing for voice(s) from the beginning of his compositional career contributed to his often-noted ability to construct singable melodies.

According to Clarke, Willan first experienced orchestral music in 1901. He was at this time employed in Wanstead and travelled into London to attend concerts. This was no small feat. His limited financial resources meant that he could only afford to take the train to Liverpool St. station, walk the four miles to Queen's Hall, attend the concert, walk back to the station, take the train to Stratford, and walk an additional six miles home (Clarke 1983, 9–10). Despite these challenges, he began to organize and conduct performances of large choral/orchestral compositions in Wanstead, and, after he moved to St. John the Baptist in London, continued to conduct the Wanstead Choral Society in such performances.[2] He also made his first attempts at orchestral composition.

In some ways Willan's style was especially well suited to orchestral or wind band music. He was an accomplished contrapuntalist. The polyphonic nature of his music, whether involving simple imitation, multiple simultaneous melodic strands, or fully developed fugue, was well suited to the use of contrasted instrumental colours. For example, the distinctive timbres of the woodwind instruments are particularly effective in pointing up imitative entries, either as soloists or in combination with other woodwinds or with strings.

On the other hand, Willan's training in England around the beginning of the twentieth century led him toward a particular concept of orchestral writing. Orchestral music by prominent English composers of the time—Hubert Parry, Charles Villiers Stanford, Arnold Bax, and Edward Elgar among others—tended toward the use of blended rather than "pure" timbres and textures; that is, these composers generally used relatively few solo or duet timbres in favour of thicker textures with considerable doubling. They also tended to prefer to emphasize the middle tessituras in the orchestral register, producing overall a warm, unified timbre. Following these procedures gave Willan's music its recognizable "Englishness," and while he availed himself of all the textural and timbral options inherent in a full orchestra setting, he never abandoned the English affinity for blended orchestral colours and richly cohesive timbres.

Several of Willan's friends reported that he felt unsure of his orchestrational skills. He did turn to others for assistance on some occasions. Apparently, Ettore Mazzoleni provided assistance with the final scoring of Symphony No. 2 and Godfrey Ridout orchestrated *A Marching Tune*. Ridout believed that Willan's orchestrations depended too heavily on the strings and therefore became monochromatic (Clarke 1983, 110, 272–73). Conversely, two conductors intimately familiar with his symphonies felt otherwise. Reginald Stewart,[3] who conducted the premiere of Symphony No. 1 in 1936, was of the opinion that Willan had an "innate instinct" for the effective use of instruments, and Walter Susskind, whose 1958 performance of Symphony No. 2 was much appreciated by the composer, felt that it was a "most satisfying work" and pointed to the originality of the rhythmic structure (especially in the Scherzo) and the colourful deployment of the wind instruments. Clarke believes that Willan's scorings do work, especially for his own music, and compares them to those of Brahms, which were often criticized for their "sameness" but are now seen as appropriate to his own compositional style (Clarke 1983, 272–74).

1
Early Orchestral Works

Prior to 1911, Willan undertook the composition of at least twelve orchestral works. He fully completed only two of these projects (one very short) and finished another in short score. The other works remained in various stages of incompleteness. That Willan left so many works unfinished is probably a consequence of his workload in England. As noted earlier, he always held an important church job, usually as both organist and choir director, taught some students (piano, organ, harmony, counterpoint), presented organ recitals, conducted outside ensembles such as community choirs, and led theatrical groups in musical productions. Such engagements likely left him little time for composition of anything other than works directly related to his professional responsibilities, and made orchestral composition, where the possibilities of performance were unsure, a luxury to which he could not dedicate much time. Nonetheless, the number of projects initiated indicates a keen interest in this genre, and the sketches that survive show a fertile imagination and a far from rudimentary understanding of how to structure large-scale orchestral compositions. Willan did not forget these early efforts. In later years he frequently borrowed thematic material and harmonic ideas from them for later compositions, although he inevitably improved on the originals in their new settings.

[Allegro marcato], HWC 65

Willan's earliest extant orchestral work is untitled, bearing only the tempo/style directive *Allegro marcato* and the completion date of March 6, 1904 (Bryant 1972, 41). This very short piece, complete, but only nine measures long, is scored for small orchestra (fl, ob, clar, bsn, 2hrn, b. trbn, pno, strings) and consists of a thirteen-voice canon on a Bach-like subject.

Example 1.1: *[Allegro marcato]*, bars 1–5

For the first few bars the subject enters on every beat, quickly generating a complex contrapuntal texture. All entries of the five-bar subject are identical, with the exception of the viola, which is transposed up a minor third. Following its iteration of the subject, each voice sustains the pitch C, again with the exception of viola on E-flat. The final three bars are mostly sustained C (viola E-flat) while the later entries of the subject complete their statement. When the final voice (bass trombone) finishes its statement, the piece ends.

Harmonically, the entire piece is a prolongation of a C minor chord, supplemented with passing harmonies. Simple though it is, this tiny work does represent a substantial contrapuntal accomplishment. Designing a subject that would permit this many superimposed entries and maintain a workable harmonic structure is a considerable challenge. Willan also demonstrated that he was cognizant of issues pertaining to orchestral balance. The first two notes of each entry are accented and the volume of the last few statements is increased to ensure audibility.

The circumstances that generated this minuscule composition are difficult to imagine. One wonders if perhaps it was some kind of joke, or a genial compositional challenge among friends, similar to the one that resulted in Dmitri Shostakovich's *Tahiti Trot*.[1] The rather dramatic nature of the music might also suggest an opening of some sort, perhaps a concert or the curtain-raising in a theatrical production, although its brevity militates against effective use in concert, and counterpoint of this complexity seems unsuited to theatre music.

Epilogue, HWC 67

The only other orchestral work that Willan fully completed in England is *Epilogue*, completed on May 19, 1909, and scored for full orchestra with harp and organ (Bryant 1972, 41). Like the brief piece just discussed, the origin of this composition is obscure. It exists in the National Library of Canada in holograph full score and parts, perhaps indicating that the composer expected a performance. These materials however are free of performer's markings, probably indicating that the prospective performance never materialized (Clarke 1983, 108–9) and that the work is still awaiting its premiere. The composition's title, scoring (presence of organ), and general style (full orchestra scoring and brass fanfares) suggest the finale of a major church event. Also, the work is based on the plainsong hymn *Urbs beata Hierusalem* (Clarke 1983, 109), the first two phrases of which are quoted in the initial bars. This hymn is associated with the dedication of a church (Frere 1909, 357–59). There is no evidence of such an event in Willan's biography at this time, but, as an experienced church musician, he would certainly have been aware of this association. Clarke observes that Willan was the organist for the Guild of All Souls and the English Church Union, who presented a couple of large-scale festivals each year. Willan apparently organized these events, conducted the music, and trained the choir (Clarke 1983, 12). Perhaps *Epilogue* was intended for one of these festivals, although if this was the case one wonders about the absence of voices.

The work opens with statements of the first two phrases of the hymn: the first is in unison in low winds and organ; the second is harmonized in the strings. This leads directly into a fanfare in brass and woodwinds (with a few interjections by the strings) that lasts for thirty-three bars. The hymn provides practically all of the musical material. The first four pitches of phrase one (three descending whole steps followed by an ascending whole step—D, C, B-flat, C) are quoted directly, transposed, rhythmically altered, and set in imitation. The descending minor third that is characteristic of phrase two is an important element of the

Example 1.2: *Epilogue*, bars 1–4

melodic construction. References to the hymn can be identified in virtually every bar. The key is ostensibly G minor, but as is usual with Willan, the harmony is modally inflected and largely non-functional.

After this substantial introduction, section one begins at bar 39. The tempo is increased from *Adagio* to *Andante maestoso*, the metre changed from 4/4 to 3/4, and a fourteen-bar melody (theme 1A) is developed from motives from the hymn, especially the three descending whole steps in the first phrase.[2] Clear references to the hymn can also be observed in the primary contrapuntal line, which is often in coupled compound thirds or sixths with the melody. Willan immediately begins to develop this melody through modulation, fragmentation, and motivic alteration. The texture is also systematically thickened.

Example 1.3: *Epilogue*, bars 39–52

A new melody (theme 1B), which appears at bar 81, is a rhythmically altered variation on theme 1A. This melody, however, is sixteen bars long and falls into regular four-bar phrases.

Example 1.4: *Epilogue*, bars 81–88

Willan also develops this theme, most notably in a descending chromatic version set against a rising chromatic bass line at bars 101–5. This section climaxes in a *fugato* on the first motive from theme 1A starting at bar 114; however, theme 1B also returns, appearing over sustained chords and a textural reduction. Section one ends with a short chorale in low brass functioning as a structural articulation—a fingerprint[3] in Willan's orchestral music.

Section two commences very quietly at bar 133. The tempo is slowed to *Andante cantabile* and the key becomes D major, although, as before, the harmony does not adhere strictly to this tonality. Willan creates a new melody (theme 2) that contrasts with theme 1, but also relates to it through intervallic content,[4] creating both contrast and unity. Uneven phrase lengths and brief woodwind solos further set this section apart from what has preceded it.

Example 1.5: *Epilogue*, bars 137–54

In developing his new melody, Willan immediately builds a *fugato* on the first two bars of the tune and also generates new material through the manipulation of other motives drawn from it. At measure 170, he reintroduces the first phrase of theme 1A against the continuing development of theme 2 as a means of preparing for a modulation back to the initial key with theme 1A at its original pitches at bar 182. This transition manages to look both forward and backward—a characteristic of transitional material that will be repeatedly encountered in Willan's orchestral music.

With the simultaneous return of the first key and theme 1A, section three, beginning at bar 182, has the sense of recapitulation. However, only the first few bars of theme 1A are precisely restated; then the composer begins harmonic development of melodic fragments. Theme 1B is also partly restated, and, like the end of section one, the accompaniment to this melody quickly simplifies to sustained chords and a textural reduction, leading to the conclusion of this section with a low brass chorale and a timpani solo.

Section four begins at bar 212. The tempo is further slowed to *Largamente* to create a majestic style as the piece moves toward its conclusion. Another new melody is developed from the first notes of the hymn.

Example 1.6: *Epilogue*, bars 212–16

While this new idea is the basis of this section, perhaps more important musically is an extended fanfare in woodwinds, brass, and organ that is also related to the hymn and contributes greatly to the imposing character of this section.

The Coda, at bar 240, is back in 4/4 and directly quotes the first three bars of the fanfare from the introduction, providing a sort of arch form. The chord progression from these earlier bars (E-flat major, F major, G minor) in intensified rhythm is used as an isorhythmic ostinato in horns and trombones, driving the music forward to a dramatic final cadence in B-flat major.

Epilogue illustrates that in this early work Willan had learned to structure orchestral pieces or movements through thematic integration, melodic and motivic development, and the use of scoring and textural accumulation and recession to define climaxes and formal divisions. The piece displays a number of Willan fingerprints, including uneven phrase structure, modally inflected and non-functional harmony that touches on many keys but does not settle on any of them, and effective melodic construction. This work, although now more than a century old, appears to have not yet been performed. It deserves re-examination and perhaps inclusion on today's orchestral programs.

Through Darkness into Light, HWC 66

The only other orchestral work completed by Willan in England is the symphonic poem *Through Darkness into Light*. The composer, however, left this work in short score, albeit with numerous scoring cues throughout that suggest a large orchestra. While the score was completed on March 10, 1908, it was not orchestrated until 1980 (by Godfrey Ridout),[5] twelve years after the composer's death (Clarke 1983, 107). The score carries the dedication "In Memoriam Denis O'Sullivan, 1 February, 1908" (Bryant 1972, 41). This apparently refers to the Irish-American operatic baritone Denis O'Sullivan, who was born in San Francisco in 1868 and died on February 1, 1908, in Columbus, Ohio. O'Sullivan pursued his career in both England and the United States, and was widely admired for his phrasing and enunciation (Sadie 1988, 548). It is not clear how Willan might have known him, but he may well have heard O'Sullivan perform in London and held the impressive singer in high esteem. Willan's dedication may be his acknowledgement of O'Sullivan's accomplishments rather than a reflection of a personal friendship.

After a slow introduction, Willan introduces the Irish folksong *Jimmy mo mhíle stór* (Jimmy, my thousand treasures) as an English horn solo. The entire tune is used, and, since it appears to be related to very little else in the symphonic poem (except to be repeated during the final climax), seems rather incongruous in context. It is difficult to avoid speculating that its inclusion was intended to reflect the Irish heritage of the dedicatee; however, O'Sullivan died on February 1, 1908, and Willan completed the work on March 10. Much of this piece must have been written before O'Sullivan's death. It seems likely, therefore, that Willan realized after the fact that his symphonic poem was an appropriate memorial to O'Sullivan and added the dedication when he heard of the singer's death. Clarke observes that Hamilton Harty used this folk song in his *Irish Symphony* of 1904, and that Willan may have heard it and been attracted to the tune (Clarke 1983, 107), but this is also speculation. The tune has musical elements that might also have attracted Willan. Its phrasing is irregular (the song is twenty-three bars long, mostly in five-bar phrases) and it is bimodal (primarily in B minor, but D major is implied as well).

This work appears to have six sections (Clarke 1983, 107–8), with a considerable amount of related material from section to section. The opening *Lento e solenne* functions like a slow introduction. Twenty-seven bars long, it is underscored throughout by a drum rhythm, presumably for timpani, that suggests a funeral march.

Example 1.7: *Through Darkness into Light*, bars 1–2

Nominally in B minor, but harmonized modally over the drum ostinato, the entire section consists of a series of chordal passages that Willan suggests be scored for woodwinds. The chords are mostly in closed position and in the low register, indicating that this music represents the "darkness" mentioned in the title. Toward the end of this section, two low-register melodic fragments emerge that quote the opening notes of the upcoming Irish folk song, one of the few instances in this work of material related to the song.

Example 1.8: *Through Darkness into Light*, bars 22–23

Section two is entirely taken up with the quotation of *Jimmy mo mhíle stór* (Jimmy, my thousand treasures). As noted earlier, this is an English horn solo over a spare accompaniment of short notes. Willan indicates a string accompaniment, presumably *pizzicato*,[6] and apparently intended to evoke a folksinger accompanying him/herself on guitar. A countermelody for viola is inserted under the last five bars of the tune.

Example 1.9: *Through Darkness into Light*, bars 28–51

The subsequent section (*Agitato e poco piu mosso*) forms a dramatic contrast to earlier music. Textures rapidly accumulate, the harmony becomes chromatic (including parallel descending chromatic chords at bars 69–73), and an underlying syncopated rhythm contributes momentum. A new motive appears in the third bar that will be extensively developed in this section and recalled repeatedly throughout the composition, becoming the principal motivic idea (A1) of most of the rest of the work. This motive, in both prime form and in inversion, is present almost constantly throughout this section and ultimately appears in *stretto* as the section reaches its climax.

Example 1.10: *Through Darkness into Light*, bars 53–54 (A1)

Section four (*Allegro feroce*) continues the development of the A1 motive. The key signature is that of C major, but the music consists of streams of unresolved diminished-seventh chords making this section essentially atonal. A new motive (B1) emerges that is derived from the first notes of the folk song.

Willan states this motive only three times then merges it into a theme that he also used in his Prelude and Fugue in C Minor written for organ

Example 1.11: *Through Darkness into Light*, bars 105–8 (B1)

in the same year (1908) (Clarke 1983, 108). Sequential development of all three motives comprises the material of this section, generating a very complex texture.

Example 1.12: *Through Darkness into Light*, bars 116–17

Toward the end of section four, Willan introduces several quick tempo changes. An *Allegro molto* that consists of the arpeggiation of a B diminished-seventh chord leads to an abrupt *Largo* with the A1 motive in the bass and, ultimately, a pounding chord in fourths and a timpani roll that bring this section to a close.

Section five (*Largo*) begins with a short reference to the drum rhythm in section one, the first time it has been associated with any music other than the introductory woodwind chords. In the second bar, A1 bursts in as a melodic/harmonic wedge in B major, gloriously representing "light," the other aspect mentioned in the title (Clarke 1983, 108).

Example 1.13: *Through Darkness into Light*, bars 164–67

This section initially contrasts third-related key areas (B major–E-flat major–C major) but ultimately becomes chromatic. The A1 motive is featured throughout in various rhythmic guises, in augmentation and in *stretto*. The E-flat major segment is taken up with a completely unexpected scoring idea. The A1 motive is extended to seven bars by six solo violins ascending into their highest register to create an ethereal texture—the light of Heaven, one presumes. Overall, this section is affirming music with a compelling forward impetus. The ending is interesting. The tempo suddenly becomes *Allegro* (bar 222) and presents the A1 wedge from the beginning of the section, but in C major, promptly repeated in B major. The effect is breathtaking and structurally convincing. A striking series of sustained major chords, which imply a *ritardando*, prepares for the next section.

The final section (*Molto maestoso*) has two subsections. Curiously, the initial subsection introduces a new melody that does not appear to be related to anything else in the piece. It has some characteristics of a folk song, but, as Clarke points out, its range comprises two full octaves, making it unlikely to be an actual folk melody (Clarke 1983, 108).

Example 1.14: *Through Darkness into Light*, bars 250–60

Eleven bars long, this section is supported by well-designed three-part counterpoint and is repeated and extended to transition to the next subsection and the climax of the work, which is a grand full-orchestra restatement of *Jimmy mo mhíle stór* (Jimmy, my thousand treasures). Willan extends the ends of each phrase in order to insert a reference to the drum rhythm from section one.[7] A short coda based on A1 and the drum rhythm completes the composition.

Willan achieved rather mixed success with *Through Darkness into Light*. On one hand the materials used are attractive, the development of themes is imaginative, some of the harmonies are as advanced as the composer would use in any of his compositions, and several extended passages generate a compelling sense of momentum and musical energy. However, the rigidly sectionalized nature of the piece creates a disjointed effect overall, especially when the two major melodies employed have little or no relation to other material. Ridout, in his "revision and orchestration," recognized these problems and tried to address them, writing, for example, a substantial transition between sections two and three based on motives from *Jimmy mo mhíle stór*. In some ways it might be said that the piece would be stronger without the Irish folk song. However, as Willan's only completed symphonic poem, it shows that he understood the form, but perhaps needed more experience to work successfully with it.

[Lento mistico], HWC 87 (unfinished)

This work is undated and untitled except for the above tempo/style indicator that only applies to the first section, or introduction. It is in full score and does not appear to be a sketch since there are very few erasures, cross-outs, or other revisions. The score abruptly ends at the last bar of page seventeen, which almost certainly indicates that pages are missing. A very large orchestra is employed. In addition to the standard complement, the scoring includes piccolo, cor anglais, bass clarinet, contra bassoon, and harp.

[Lento mistico] is one of the early works from which Willan would borrow extensively, in this case for the third movement of his Symphony No. 1, written in the mid-1930s. Although left incomplete, the music apparently remained important to the composer, and he was able to reuse it effectively when his skills as an orchestral composer had been substantially refined.

The opening section or introduction, *Lento mistico*, comprises one of the "mystical choruses" that Willan wrote so well and used so effectively throughout his career. The key is presumably E major, but the harmony is non-functional and includes many unresolved sevenths. After four bars, the string parts are simplified to a sustained E major chord, while the woodwinds, solo cello, and horns contribute short melodic figures, most of which enter on non-harmonic tones, adding to the unsettled feeling of the music. At bar thirteen, solo horn presents a more extended melody accompanied by slow-moving string chords. Both the solos and the chords are important building blocks for the rest of the composition. Curiously, during the horn solo the tempo is suddenly increased to

Example 1.15: *[Lento mistico]*, bars 13–20 (horn solo)

Poco allegro without any apparent change of style, an awkward gesture perhaps indicating that this is among Willan's earliest orchestral projects. The introduction ends very quietly with disjunct C-sharp minor seventh chords in the strings and a hushed timpani roll.

Section one at bar 23, *Allegro*, is in dramatic contrast to the dreamy music of the introduction. Chromatic lines in strings and woodwinds sweep upward while a motive from the horn solo is developed imitatively and through fragmentation and recombination. At bars 32–34 a chromatic sixteenth-note passage rises swiftly through the strings. Willan employs such passages frequently in his orchestral music as beginnings or to define formal divisions.[8] In this case, the "rush" ushers in a new melodic idea, drawn from an oboe solo during the introduction, which Willan develops in similar fashion to the previous segment and expands to considerable length.[9]

Example 1.16: *[Lento mistico]*, bars 35–38

Although no actual formal division is specified, there appears to be a new section beginning at bar 54. The texture and surface rhythms are simplified, a new thematic fragment is introduced that is again developed from introductory motives, and a distinctive series of chords from the introduction reappears. The melodic motive is quickly developed through imitation, and gradually other earlier motives are integrated into the counterpoint, building up a progressively more complex texture that has substantial forward momentum. The music comes to an abrupt end at bar 92 in what is clearly not the conclusion of the piece.

It appears that this work is one of Willan's earliest undertakings in orchestral composition. Even though this score is apparently not a sketch—that is, it seems to be the ultimate result of previous drafts—transitions between sections and subsections are often abrupt and awkward, and some of the scoring, especially where important melodic lines are fragmented and scattered through several contrasting instrumental timbres, is of doubtful workability. On the other hand, the piece holds together well since all of the melodic material has a common germ and generally involves rapidly ascending scalic and chromatic lines. Much of the counterpoint is well conceived and effective. Together the melodic profiles and the counterpoint combine to generate high energy. Certainly, Willan had the musical material here for a compelling orchestral work,[10] although his inexperience in writing for the genre is also evident. One can only imagine what the composer might have done with this material given the time to undertake further development and refinement.

Rhapsody "From the Highlands," HWC 85 (unfinished)

This work, which exists only in short score, has a date, August 1911, on the title page (Bryant 1972, 44). In its incomplete state it is difficult to determine what Willan might have done with it, although a few scoring cues here and there give some indication of his thoughts. For example, the work opens with a long, slow introduction with tremolo chords, apparently intended for strings, supporting a lyrical English horn solo and a number of low-register, fanfare-like melodic fragments. Another English horn solo later on includes (not surprisingly) the Scotch snap,[11] generating a folk-like context.

The first section, *Allegro feroce*, presents a theme that would be reused and recomposed as the primary theme of the first movement of Symphony No. 1. In its counterpoint it displays an interesting 3 against 2 hemiola that is developed in this work and would be carried over in a similar fashion to Symphony No. 1. A second section offers a new lyrical theme that is specified for viola. The theme is canonic, but no instrument is specified for the answer. Perhaps Willan intended that both parts be played by violas.

Early Orchestral Works   37

Example 1.17: *Rhapsody "From the Highlands,"* bars 69–71

Willan produced more than 200 bars of this work in short score, a considerable effort. In its unfinished state it would not normally be of particular interest, except that it is, in effect, a partial sketch for Symphony No. 1.

Overture, HWC 91a (unfinished)

Unlike the other works reviewed thus far, this Overture does not include a slow introduction, but begins *Allegro vivace* with a "Willan rush"—sixteenth notes rising rapidly from low to high strings. Many other Willan works begin in similar fashion.

Although undated, this work is in full score (sixty-five bars) and includes a quotation from Walt Whitman: "Know'st thou the excellent joys of youth." The opening string rush gives way to fanfares in trumpets and trombones and later to a *Maestoso* horn call that was used verbatim as the second motive of the third movement of Symphony No. 1. When the *Allegro vivace* returns, a new horn call appears that is developed imitatively, appears in virtually every bar, and is moved effectively through the instruments to generate momentum and varied timbre.

Example 1.18: Overture, bars 20–22

The piece then dwindles out to single melodic strands based on both horn calls.

Although it never got beyond the initial stages of creation, this work does show some evolution in Willan's compositional skill in writing for orchestra, especially in relation to scoring. And, as has been observed of many of these early orchestral works, the composer returned to it for melodic material later in his career.

Other Unfinished Works[12]

In addition to the works reviewed above, Willan also worked on two other orchestral pieces at this time.[13] The symphonic poems *The Call of the Sea*, HWC 88, and *Seaside Elegiacs*, HWC 89, exist as rough sketches with many erasures, revisions, and cross-outs, making it impossible to determine much about their concept and ultimate realization. They do include several pleasant melodies that offered potential for effective development, and hints of interesting scoring. Willan also reused material from *The Call of the Sea* in his *Hymn to the Sun* (1930) for chorus and orchestra (Clarke 1983, 94).

These early orchestral works illustrate that Willan's musical imagination at this point in his career extended well beyond commitments to his professional engagements. That he left so many of these projects unfinished is, as previously noted, probably attributable to his workload and his growing familial responsibilities. Certainly, analysis of these scores demonstrates that he had enough musical materials to create at least a couple of viable, well-constructed works. One cannot but wonder, however, about the number of undertakings initiated. Why did Willan start so many projects, only to leave them unfinished, instead of concentrating his available efforts on one or two that could be completed? Ultimately, of course, by taking a broader approach he was able to note down, at least fragmentarily, a considerable number of intriguing ideas that would serve him well in later, more accomplished compositions.

2
Works for Small Orchestra

Willan's oeuvre includes few works for chamber orchestra. Incidental music for theatrical productions at Hart House during the 1920s and others such as *Nativity Play* and *Brébeuf* comprise the majority of his compositions scored for small orchestra. While undoubtedly effective in their original context, they are by and large unsuited for concert performance. In addition, in 1931 Willan wrote *Three Dances*, HWC 68, for small orchestra, but the score and almost all of the parts have been lost. All that survives is an oboe part that displays performer's markings indicating that the work was completed and performed (Bryant 1972, 41). One can only hope that the performance materials, or at least the score, of this work might be recovered; a composition like this by Willan would be a boon to conductors of chamber orchestras.

Overture to *The Alchemist*, HWC 4

Willan's theatre music did produce one short piece that could profitably enter the Canadian chamber orchestra repertoire—the overture to the 1920 production of Ben Jonson's *The Alchemist*. This bright, melodious work stands well on its own[1] but has never been published and is only available in manuscript from the National Library of Canada.[2] The music Willan wrote for *The Alchemist* is simple but energetic and tuneful. Despite its straightforward materials, the Overture is well constructed and an excellent example of the composer's ability to create fine melodies and submit them to imaginative development.

Willan's resources at Hart House were obviously limited. The orchestra employed in the music for *The Alchemist* comprises strings and two woodwinds—flute and clarinet. Despite the nominal instrumentation, Willan makes effective use of his limited means. The nine-bar slow introduction that opens the Overture is, in effect, a recitative for solo flute (the "flute motive").

Example 2.1: Overture to *The Alchemist*, bars 1–9

Opening a dramatic production with a solo instrument, especially one of constrained volume like the flute, seems unusual in a context where more robust beginnings are the norm; however, it was perhaps appropriate for a play dealing with magic and the exotic, especially when combined (as it is here) with melodic tritones and harmony featuring unresolved diminished sevenths, added-note chords, and augmented triads.[3] The flute takes the lead throughout these measures but is imitated by first violin and later by clarinet, cello, and other strings. The texture is gradually thickened, primarily by doubling the melodic fragments, particularly by clarinet. Overall, this introduction projects a sense of mystery and unpredictability appropriate to the theme and action of the play.

The *Con brio* that comprises most of the Overture begins promptly at bar 10. Willan presents two appealing melodies, then blends together both themes and the "flute motive" in what might be labelled a "development section." His skill at fragmenting melodies, recombining motives, and varying the scoring maintains energy and musical interest even though the materials used are much simpler than those seen in earlier works.

Theme 1 is five bars long. After the theme has been stated, Willan doesn't precisely repeat it but extracts motives and adds a canonic presentation of the flute motive to complete an "A" section of fourteen bars. Willan's penchant for unusual phrase lengths runs through all of his music, including this rather simple music intended for the theatre.

Example 2.2: Overture to *The Alchemist*, bars 10–14

The "B" section begins at bar 24 with a new theme that consists of (rather unusually for Willan) four four-bar phrases.

Example 2.3: Overture to *The Alchemist*, bars 24–39

After a single presentation of the complete theme, the "development section" begins at bar 40. In the first subsection of development, the

42   This Awareness of Beauty

Example 2.4: Overture to *The Alchemist*, bars 40–48

woodwinds and the strings alternate on canonic statements of the flute motive, which is later combined with hints of theme 2.

In the second subsection, beginning at bar 59, the opening motive of theme 1 is recalled and blended with a derivation of theme 2, while other voices (principally the strings) generate additional contrapuntal strands. Two bars of silence separate the development from a restatement that recaps the first thirteen bars of the *Con brio*.

In the score as it stands, the tempo is then abruptly reduced to *Andante*, and the final few bars of the introduction are repeated to prepare for the first scene of the play. For a concert performance, a conductor could easily insert the final four bars of act 1 at bar 86 of the Overture to provide a secure cadence. As Clarke has observed, "this overture is a well-written, well-integrated, and charming piece of music" (Clarke 1983, 149). Conductors of chamber orchestras will find many rewards behind its simple, tuneful facade.

Overture to an Unwritten Comedy, HWC 79

Willan's only other extant work for comparatively small orchestra is the *Overture to an Unwritten Comedy*, one of his most frequently performed compositions.[4] Written in 1951 and scored for flute, oboe, clarinet,

Example 2.5: Overture to *The Alchemist*, bars 59–67

bassoon, pairs of horns, trumpets and trombones, timpani, harp, and strings, it carries the dedication: "To my old friend, John Adaskin, with whom I have often exchanged a merry quip and prank, this work is affectionately inscribed." A considerably more sophisticated work, compositionally and in terms of orchestration, than the Overture to *The Alchemist*, it illustrates that Willan's substantial experience writing for orchestra gained during the 1930s and 40s resulted in fluent handling of his musical materials and substantial imagination in the varied use of the instruments.

The work sounds English. The strings play virtually continuously, present much of the melodic material, and are often doubled by the woodwinds and (to a lesser extent) by the brass. Very few range extremes appear in any instrument, and the only solo texture is a short passage for four string soloists (bars 45–50). The main theme is an expressive, folk-like melody reminiscent of similar tunes by Elgar or Holst, although its cheerful, even exuberant, character differs from the grand, ceremonial melodies of Willan's English compatriots.

The piece opens briskly with an eleven-bar introduction presenting lively music that will be recalled and developed throughout the composition. Perhaps most notable is a rapid sixteenth-note passage that descends through the strings, an inverted "Willan rush." Theme 1, the English-style "big tune," appears at bar 12, establishing the "A" section of the piece.[5]

Example 2.6: *Overture to an Unwritten Comedy*, bars 12–19

Interestingly, when Willan repeats this tune he extends it to nine bars without any apparent awkwardness in the periodic structure. Transition begins immediately. The first transitional motive, which will also be recalled from time to time, is a bright figure played by the woodwinds accompanied only by rhythmically disjunct chords in harp and pizzicato strings.

Example 2.7: *Overture to an Unwritten Comedy*, bars 28–31

An interesting scoring idea in this passage places the flute below the oboe and sometimes below the clarinet as well. Willan apparently wanted to emphasize the "reedy" quality of the oboe on the melody, or wanted to darken the overall timbre by blending the flute colour into the overall woodwind sound.

The second transitional motive is longer and harmonically complex. The main purpose of this motive is to effect a modulation from D major to B-flat major in preparation for the B section, but before that happens the first transitional motive returns, transposed down a minor third, leading to a fermata that indicates the end of the A section.

Example 2.8: *Overture to an Unwritten Comedy*, bars 32–39

The B section commences at bar 45 in B-flat major with the solo string passage identified earlier. Although not indicated in the score, a tradition of playing these bars at a slower tempo in performance has evolved over the years in the numerous performances this work has received and seems very much in character with the music. When theme 2 arrives at bar 50, the original tempo is usually re-established. Theme 2 is rhythmically related to the first transitional motive, and Willan scored it in a similar fashion—woodwinds with a simple string and harp accompaniment.

Example 2.9: *Overture to an Unwritten Comedy*, bars 50–53

The connection with the first transitional motive is further solidified when the second transitional motive, with some alteration, promptly follows theme 2. This appearance of the second transitional motive leads the music back to D major but is also considerably extended by a reiteration of theme 2 decorated with a lively sixteenth-note counterpoint that derives from the introduction. The B section concludes with a restatement of the inverted Willan rush that completed the introduction. Reintroducing motives from the introduction in this manner is an intuitive means of preparing for the return of the A section, which follows immediately. The transition from B to A is seamlessly accomplished.

The rest of the work is a recapitulation of the A section but with some of the motives transposed and generally thicker in texture. Willan cleverly inserts a brief reference to theme 2 at bars 108–9, immediately preceding the Coda. The Coda is short and begins with another iteration of the inverted Willan rush from the introduction, but the composer provides yet another surprise. The final three bars of the piece are *Maestoso* and present an unexpected chord progression, perhaps intended as a fleeting reminder of the key of the B section—B-flat major.[6]

Example 2.10: *Overture to an Unwritten Comedy*, bars 112–14

Overture to an Unwritten Comedy is one of Willan's most successful orchestral works, in terms of both the facility demonstrated by its composition and its popular appeal. Interesting material developed skilfully, a joyful character, and deft scoring have ensured it an enduring place in the Canadian orchestral repertoire.

3

Shorter Orchestral Works

Willan's shorter orchestral compositions[1] were mostly written for special ceremonial or patriotic occasions, which, of course, largely determined their style. Two of these works were intended for celebrations related to the British royal family and adopted the style of British ceremonial music of the early twentieth century. Willan was proud of his British heritage and was undoubtedly pleased to be able to contribute to these festivities (Clarke 1983, 34, 50, 61). Also included in this genre are two arrangements that are orchestrations by the composer of works originally written for other media. One of these arrangements, *Poem for String Orchestra*, is among Willan's most accomplished compositions.

Coronation March (Marche solennelle), HWC 71

Willan's *Coronation March* was written to commemorate the coronation of George VI and Queen Elizabeth in 1937 (Clarke 1983, 109). He had begun working on the march nearly a year earlier and had completed a short score by the end of October 1936. The full score was not completed until June 7, 1937, almost a month after the coronation had taken place.[2] The first performance took place very shortly after the completion of the full score, on July 1, 1937. Reginald Stewart conducted the Toronto Promenade Symphony Orchestra (Bryant 1972, 42). In the years following the premiere, the work was well received.

Willan's autograph score, a copy of which is in the Canadian Music Centre, Toronto, lists fifteen performances between 1937 and 1953, including one by the BBC in London on July 1, 1942. Since that time, the work has attracted considerably less interest among conductors. Canada has become much more multicultural since the 1950s, and the audience for works like this, in English style and connected with a British political event, has been considerably reduced since the middle decades of the twentieth century.

Not surprisingly, the piece follows the model of British ceremonial marches in style and form; however, Willan also adds unique aspects to each section of the form. Perhaps most notable is the long, slow introduction, but, as will be seen, unexpected elements appear regularly throughout the composition. The first thirteen bars are a fanfare for brass and timpani. A quiet timpani roll begins the work, a musical gesture often used to open Willan's orchestral compositions. The fanfare first appears in horns, then in trumpets. Interestingly, while the key of the piece is seemingly B-flat major and the timpani plays a long tonic pedal, the brass fanfares do not conform to this key.[3] The horn statement establishes E-flat major and the trumpet answer is in G-flat major, creating a pleasing series of harmonic third relationships set against the apparent tonic. The fanfare itself follows Willan's favourite approach to this medium—root-position, closed-position chords, usually major sonorities. In this case, such chords are mixed with chords in fifths. This fanfare will recur regularly throughout the march in linking passages and is a primary feature of the Coda.

The second part of the introduction is a modulatory passage based on a two-bar motive developed from the fanfare. The key throughout is highly ambiguous. Streams of first- and second-inversion and augmented chords flow over a descending chromatic bass line essentially removing any sense of tonal centre.

The first strain of the march begins at bar 28 with a three-bar "vamp" figure reminiscent of similar figures in Elgar's *Pomp and Circumstance* marches. Willan's march theme for this strain, which arrives at bar 31, contains hints of the fanfare in both melody and accompanying counterpoint. The theme comprises two four-bar phrases that are then repeated. While the tonic is ostensibly E-flat, the tonality is fluid (the first

Example 3.1: *Coronation March*, bars 3–12

phrase cadences in D major). The preference for major-chord sonorities also militates against a secure sense of key. In the third bar of each phrase the chords change much more quickly than would be expected in most march music. A brief transition, in reduced texture and based on motives from the march theme, leads to the second strain.

Willan's second strain is unusual in several ways. Instead of creating another extended marching tune, his melody is in antecedent-consequent form, divided between trumpet (antecedent) and first violins (consequent) and presented once.

Example 3.2: *Coronation March*, bars 31–39

What happens next is another surprise. Willan inserts a fourteen-bar development based on motives related to the theme from strain one and to the "Scotch snap" motive from the second strain, an insightful means of integrating both themes and unifying the two strains. The "March" section of the work is completed with one statement of the theme of the first strain[4] and a brief recall of the fanfare and the "vamp" figure, creating an arch form for this section and rounding it off in an imaginative and musically effective manner.

Example 3.3: *Coronation March*, bars 51–59

The Trio presents the requisite grand, patriotic theme. Willan's melody, however, employs uneven phrase lengths (not the customary structure for such themes) and includes brief chorale-like inserts by harp and celeste between the phrases. These inserts generate striking aural events, but also prepare for the Coda, where this theme will be restated in grandiose style with trumpet fanfares and bell sequences replacing the harp and celeste on the interphrasal inserts. The complete melody is then repeated in fuller scoring and with new contrapuntal strands.

British ceremonial marches normally include a *Da capo*, and Willan's march conforms to this structure, but with individual elements. The fanfare from the introduction is reduced to three bars; the modulatory passage to nine. The March section is repeated complete, except that the development subsection is somewhat truncated.

The Coda arrives at bar 194 in a peal of bells.[5] A brief transition leads to the expected grandiose statement of the Trio theme. Here, Willan calls for three additional trumpets that, along with the bells, provide the inserts between the phrases. However, instead of the chorale fragments previously heard, the inserted music at this point comprises three-bar motives from the fanfare and isorhythmic ostinato bell sequences, certainly spectacular additions to the music. As Elgar had done in *Pomp and Circumstance March No. 1*, Willan completes his march with an *Allegro* that features the additional trumpets and bells. An effective orchestrational idea has the fanfare tossed between the additional trumpets and those in the orchestra.

Willan's *Coronation March* is a worthy contribution to the repertoire of ceremonial marches in the British tradition. While conforming to the tradition of such works as established by Elgar and others, the composer also employed his own distinctive approach in working with musical material.

52 This Awareness of Beauty

Example 3.4: *Coronation March*, bars 87–115

Example 3.4: *Coronation March*, bars 87–115

(continues on next page)

54   This Awareness of Beauty

(continued from previous page)

Example 3.4: *Coronation March*, bars 87–115

A Marching Tune, HWC 73

A Marching Tune was written during 1941–42, in the midst of the Second World War. As noted earlier, it carries the dedication: "To all loyal gentlemen, with a special thought for the Queen's Own Rifles."[6] The work, a tribute to Canadian servicemen, was also an acknowledgement that Willan's son Bernard was serving with the Queen's Own Rifles (Clarke 1983, 110) and undoubtedly often in his father's thoughts.

Godfrey Ridout completed much of the orchestration, probably because Willan was engaged in composing the second movement of Symphony no. 2 and the music for the radio opera *Transit through Fire* (Clarke 1983, 37–38, 97). Ridout used Willan's pen and carefully copied the composer's handwriting. Without knowing in advance, one would be hard pressed to recognize the full score as anything but Willan's own original work (Clarke 1983, 110).

A Marching Tune is structured in an expanded ternary form. The A section opens with two bars of snare drum playing a military slow-march figure, which sets the mood, but seems somewhat incongruent with theme one, a long song-like melody mostly in Aeolian mode.[7] It consists of four four-bar phrases, the first three of which are presented by clarinets, the fourth by first violins, an attractive scoring idea that will be duplicated throughout the composition. As if to compensate for the non-militaristic character of the melody, various instruments insert triplet fanfare figures between the phrases.

A very brief transition leads to a full orchestra repeat of the theme. As before, the fourth phrase is entrusted to strings (in this case, violins and violas in unison), but phrase three initially appears in trumpets and trombones, another new and ear-catching timbre. A rescored statement of the earlier transition and a quiet recall of the snare drum figure prepare for the B section of the form.

The B section and theme two arrive at bar 45. The new theme contrasts with its predecessor by being in a new key and not so clearly divided into phrases. In fact, few cadences can be easily identified. Its opening has a modal character similar to theme one, but it quickly begins to wander harmonically, touching on, but not establishing, several keys. However, the two themes also have several motives in common, which, as will be seen, served Willan's purposes especially well.

Example 3.5: *A Marching Tune*, bars 3–18

    Willan does not repeat theme two, but launches a development section, which would not normally be part of ternary form. In fact, motivic development begins before the end of theme two, eliding the B section with the unexpected development. Elements of theme two provide much of the material for this section, but since the two themes share motives,

Example 3.6: *A Marching Tune*, bars 45–69

it is often not apparent which theme is being developed. The blending of the themes allows Willan to effect a masterful transition back to the A section—a compositional adroitness that has been observed in his orchestral music from his earliest works.

The repeat of the A section, a requisite of ternary form, recalls the timbres of the initial presentation but also incorporates some rescoring. After the transition has been recalled, Willan presents another surprise by restating the first part of theme two as a means of building to the work's primary climax and the beginning of the Coda (bar 141). Like the earlier development section, the Coda is mainly based on theme two, although hints of theme one are also present. The work ends dramatically in D major.

A Marching Tune is enjoyable, generally straightforward music that is rendered more interesting by Willan's expansion of the small form with which he was working. That he did not consider it among his most important compositions would seem to be confirmed by the fact that he delegated the orchestration to Ridout, but at the same time it was (and is) a heartfelt tribute to the sacrifices of servicemen and their families everywhere.

Fugue in G Minor, HWC 105

The Fugue in G Minor for strings was originally part of the incidental music for the second version of the radio play/pageant *Brébeuf*. In the late 1930s, Willan was commissioned to write music for a pageant based on the poem *Brébeuf and His Brethren*, by E.J. Pratt, which was to be presented at the Jesuit Martyrs' Shrine in Midland, Ontario. When the Second World War broke out, the project was shelved. A shortened version for radio broadcast was commissioned by the CBC in 1943 and was also performed at Massey Hall, Toronto, one year later. When a Brébeuf Festival was planned for Midland in 1947, Willan substantially expanded his original music for the pageant, inserting a number of dramatically effective elements. Unfortunately, the intended festival did not materialize and the new version was not performed until 1967 (Clarke 1983, 159).

Willan added a considerable amount of music to the score for the proposed 1947 event, including the Fugue in G Minor, which appears in section number eleven and is followed by his 1943 choral setting of *Ave verum corpus*, which uses the same theme. Willan seems to have been proud of this music. The *Ave verum corpus* was published as an independent sacred motet in 1948, and the Fugue reappeared in 1951 as part of the Prelude and Fugue movement of *Three Pieces for Organ* (Clarke 1983, 161, 238). Willan also extracted the Fugue for performance as a string quartet or, with the addition of an optional double bass part, as a work for string orchestra. This version was first performed in 1947 (Bryant 1972, 48), very shortly after its completion.

In some of the music for *Brébeuf*, Willan deliberately imitated the style of the early seventeenth century, the time when Jean de Brébeuf and his Jesuit companions were ministering to the Wendat (Huron) First Nation in central Ontario. The Fugue has the character of the baroque in its linear elements, but in the harmony Willan's fondness for modal inflection, wandering key structures, and augmented chords brings it into the twentieth century. The subject consists of only four notes.

Willan wrote a real answer, which began stretching the key immediately. There is no actual countersubject; however, the brief figure that accompanies the answer, with its chromaticism and distinctive octave skip, recurs in various modifications throughout this short work. Most

Example 3.7: Fugue in G Minor, bars 1–4

of the contrapuntal practices associated with baroque fugal technique are present. The first episode includes *stretto*; a section of free counterpoint makes reference to both the subject and the rudimentary countersubject; and, at the work's climax, the subject appears in inversion in first violin, which is set against itself on its original pitches in the bass line and a slightly altered version of the "countersubject" in second violin.

The Fugue in G Minor is primarily a work for string quartet; however, with judicious doublings and the provided optional double bass part, it can be successfully included on a string orchestra concert. Independent of its original theatrical context, its style seems startling in relation to Willan's other works and is unique in his orchestral output. However, many twentieth-century composers have engaged with the neoclassical movement, recloaking past styles in modern garb, as Willan has accomplished in this piece. Although not among his usual procedures, at least within his orchestral music, it illustrates that he was as capable as anyone in revisiting older traditions and viewing them through contemporary eyes.

Royal Salute, HWC 80

Willan's *Royal Salute* was commissioned by the CBC to commemorate the visit to Canada by Queen Elizabeth II in the summer of 1959. The work was completed on May 24, 1959, and was first performed a few weeks later on June 17. Geoffrey Waddington conducted the CBC Toronto Orchestra (Bryant 1972, 43).

Since they were intended for similar purposes, *Royal Salute* and *Coronation March* have a number of points in common, although *Royal Salute* also shows the experience with orchestral composition that Willan had garnered over the twenty-two years between the coronation of

George VI and the Canadian visit by Queen Elizabeth II. While both works are structured as British ceremonial marches, *Royal Salute*, with one exception, is more tightly organized around a few well-constructed musical ideas than was its predecessor.

The first section of *Royal Salute* was borrowed from Willan's *Choral March* of 1922; however, that music had already appeared in the incidental music for *Cymbeline* (1921), which itself had been borrowed from an unfinished March in E for two pianos of 1912 (Clarke 1983, 113, 151). The piece opens with a five-bar introduction that leads directly into the first strain. The warm, lyrical music of the introduction creates an inviting mood, but, curiously, this material has no apparent connection to anything else in the composition, an unusual way for Willan to begin an orchestral work, although these introductory measures do recur at significant points in the form. The primary melody of the first strain is eight bars long and projects a spacious quality.

Example 3.8: *Royal Salute*, bars 6–13

It is not repeated as might be expected, but instead proceeds into a fifteen-bar development that uses motives from the theme and introduces new melodic elements.

The second strain arrives at bar 29 and offers several surprises. The key is transposed up a half-step (from E-flat to E), and, rather than creating a new melody, Willan continues the development initiated in the previous strain, drawing particularly on the first two bars of the primary melody of the first strain. After the second strain, the entire first strain, including the introduction, is repeated, creating a structure within the "March" section of the piece similar to that already seen in *Coronation March*.

The Trio also recalls *Coronation March*. Willan's regal tune begins by virtually quoting from his earlier work; however, in *Royal Salute* the melody is thirteen bars long, and, similar to the theme two in *A Marching Tune*, has no distinct cadences defining independent phrases.

Example 3.9: *Royal Salute*, bars 76–88

The third bar of this tune clearly recalls a motive (melody and harmony) from the comparable melody in Elgar's *Pomp and Circumstance March No. 1*. It seems unlikely that such a reference could have been accidental. Elgar's march was very well known, and he was, in many respects, the Edwardian composer par excellence, many of his works appearing when the British Empire was at its height prior to the First World War. Since Willan was developing his compositional identity at the same time, it is hardly surprising that he would look to Elgar for models when writing works associated with the British monarch, or that he would quote him in one of these compositions. It may also be instructive to note that Elgar's birthday was June 2 (Sadie 1988, 236), a few days after Willan completed *Royal Salute*.

From a compositional point of view, it is important to observe that this reference to Elgar's march had appeared earlier in *Royal Salute*—rather subtly "hidden" in the accompaniment at bars 21–22, and an excellent example of the thorough musical integration that Willan was able to accomplish at this point in his career. The Trio is completed by a repeat of the "big tune," which modulates partway through to prepare for the expected *Da capo* of the first and second strains (again including the introduction).

As is customary in works like this, the *Da capo* is followed by a majestic restatement of the Trio theme at a slower tempo, here marked *Nobilmente*. As happened in the Trio, the melody appears twice, each time in grander style. The Coda, like *Coronation March*, consists of an extended trumpet fanfare and a dramatic full-orchestra cadence, although no change of tempo is specified.

Royal Salute was undoubtedly effective in its original venue and served its purpose admirably. It is also a well-unified composition, making thorough use of limited musical materials while at the same time taking an imaginative approach to a familiar formal structure.

Poem for String Orchestra, HWC 82

Poem, one of Willan's unquestioned masterpieces for orchestra, was completed in 1959, but its gestation period had lasted for more than fifty years. This music first appeared in 1903–5 as the *Adagio* for an unfinished string quartet. Willan completed the string quartet movement in 1930 under the title *Celtic Sketches No. 1* and added the inscription "And evening, full of the linnet's wings" from the popular poem "The Lake Isle of Innisfree," by Irish poet W.B. Yeats.[8] Clarke believes Willan intended a series of "Celtic Sketches" for string quartet but finished only this one movement. He subsequently changed the title to *Poem*. In 1959, he rescored the string quartet movement for string orchestra, rewriting many of the parts, expanding the violin and viola parts through *divisi* and adding a double bass part that is often independent of the cellos (Clarke 1983, 113, 176). The new version was first performed on May 3, 1960, at the Eaton Auditorium in Toronto. Heinz Unger[9] conducted the York Concert Society Orchestra (Bryant 1972, 44).

By changing the title of the work to *Poem*, Willan may have been indicating that his music referenced all of Yeats's poem, not just the line employed as the inscription. The poem evokes a nostalgic withdrawal into seclusion in a natural environment—the island of Innisfree. This view matches the mood of Willan's music, and, as will be seen, some sections of the score appear to project programmatic images that correspond to those in the poem.

The A section, marked *Lento*, introduces the first extended melody, which is divided between the violin sections. Elements appearing in both the melody and the counterpoint will recur throughout the work, notably the opening octave skip and a series of triplet figures in second violins and violas.

Example 3.10: *Poem*, bars 1–20

A short recitative section for first violins immediately follows the completion of theme one, a pleasing change of scoring from the full orchestra textures thus far, and another element that will reappear several times. The A section is rounded off by recalling the first four bars of theme one in slightly altered rhythm, making the section a miniature arch form, an example of the thorough musical integration that characterizes this entire work.

A brief developmental transition precedes the B section. Marked slightly faster (*Poco piu mosso*), it presents textures new to this piece, including call and response—the high strings respond to the cellos—and *fugato*. Both textural events develop motives heard earlier in the piece. For example, both the cello line and the subject of the *fugato* draw on segments of the violin recitative.

The "B" section presents another long melody. Although the key signature does not change, this section seems to begin in B major, but, as is often the case in Willan's music, chromatic counterpoint quickly dissipates the sense of tonality.

The melody is supported by a rippling triplet figure that recalls parts of the accompaniment from the A section but may also be intended to represent the waves on the lake that are mentioned in Yeats's poem. Also like the A section, the B section concludes by restating the first four bars of its theme, in this case transposed down a perfect fourth and scored as a viola solo, an effective use of parallel structure between two of the main components of the work.

Example 3.11: *Poem*, bars 44–60

At this point, Willan provides a surprise. A C section, marked *Allegretto scherzando*, appears abruptly and completely changes the character of the music. The new melody sounds distinctively different from anything preceding it but is, in fact, derived directly from the two previous bars (66–67).

Example 3.12: *Poem*, bars 68–76

With its non-diatonic intervals and "chirping" motive (second half of bars 69 and 71), this melody seems to evoke birdsong. It also incorporates, and is accompanied by, chromatic triplet figures most of which are played tremolo, suggesting that Willan intended here to describe the "linnet's wings" of the inscription. These figures lead to the primary climax of the piece, a *fortissimo* C-sharp major chord under a fermata. Apparently, the evening is indeed very "full of the linnet's wings."

A short development using material from the earlier transition and the C section ensues, leading to a reversed recapitulation. The B section returns at bar 97 transposed up a major second, and using the key signature of B-flat minor, but tonic chords are difficult to find. The music gradually returns to the original key (E major) preparing for the return of theme one. Motives reminiscent of the A section appear in the accompaniment to the theme two, and hints of the B section continue into the restatement of A. As has been seen in other works, even those from very early in Willan's career, the transition to the A section is very skilfully achieved. Theme one returns at bar 113 on its original pitches, initially in cellos and basses, then in first violins. Thirteen bars of theme one are restated in intensified texture and are extended by four bars to prepare for the Coda.

The Coda (bar 130) begins with a cello solo that recalls the timbre, but not the pitches, of the first transition. While most of the music here has no direct connection to earlier material, a number of similar motives appear. The character, however, is quite different from previous sections. Willan muted the high strings, simplified the texture, and employed very quiet dynamics; although not marked in the score until the closing bars, the entire Coda could sound even more final if taken at a slower tempo. Subdued and tranquil, this highly personal music may suggest that Willan had the final line of the poem ("I hear it in the deep heart's core") in mind when he composed these measures.

Poem is "a remarkable example of the combination of youthful imagination and expression with mature craftsmanship" (Clarke 1983, 114). For a careful reader/listener the score provides virtually endless discoveries of subtle connections among the materials and expert musical development. Willan's ability to integrate every element of the music, while at the same time constantly varying his motivic material, brings both variety and unity to the work as a whole. An emotionally mature composition, *Poem* is a remarkable Canadian contribution the string orchestra repertoire.

Centennial (or Ceremonial) March, HWC 84

By the 1960s Willan had achieved the status of a national icon, through such acknowledgements as the National Film Board's short film *Man of Music* (1959), numerous honorary degrees and awards, and notable performances of his music. When the Centennial of the country's Confederation arrived in 1967, he was asked to contribute to the celebrations and responded with two works: the *Centennial Anthem*, which was performed on Parliament Hill in Ottawa on December 31, 1966, and the *Centennial March* or *Ceremonial March* (Willan used both titles), which was his last work for orchestra (Clarke 1983, 64, 66).

Throughout his life, Willan was always able to compose very quickly. However, by 1967 he was in poor health and was virtually blind. Composing the *Centennial (Ceremonial) March* was a considerable struggle. The original intention was that his march be played by professional orchestras in every region of Canada; however, by the time the march was completed (fifty-two pages of score!) the orchestral season was over, and the work received its first performance in Ottawa, August 1967, in a band transcription by Captain Charles A.W. Adams, conductor of the Canadian Guards band.[10]

For inspiration, Willan again reached back into his past—to Edward Elgar, and, in particular, to the *Pomp and Circumstance March No. 1*. Like its model, the *Centennial (Ceremonial) March* begins with an agitated first strain, which includes an energetic introduction to establish the overall character, two vigorous themes, and a recall of the first theme, creating a small ternary form with introduction.

The introduction, however, includes several Willan fingerprints. Thirteen bars long, it presents a two-bar timpani roll, followed by a modified "Willan rush" in the strings that divides into two phrases of six and four bars respectively, and elides into the first theme. Motives that will have prominent roles in the following melodic structure are easily identified in both melody and accompaniment.

The first theme, which arrives at bar 13, is structured in antecedent-consequent form. The antecedent, four bars long, is scored for clarinets and bassoons; the consequent, in the strings, is extended to seven bars. It appears twice with the texture thickened during the repeat.

Example 3.13: *Centennial (Ceremonial) March*, bars 13–23 (theme one)

Willan's transition consists of three four-bar phrases. The composer's often surprising harmonic usage can be found throughout the march, but is effectively illustrated in the first (and third) transitional phrase(s). Scored for brass only with the trumpets in their high register to emphasize the dissonance, these measures are polytonal, beginning with a D major chord, then proceeding through two polychords, G major/D major, and E minor/D major, to a dominant/tonic cadence in D major.[11] This passage certainly does not sound like Elgar.

Example 3.14: *Centennial (Ceremonial) March*, bars 37–38

The intermediate phrase is simpler harmonically, possibly to emphasize the astringency of the brass passage that precedes and follows it, and is scored for woodwinds in coupled thirds playing a motive derived from the first theme.

The second theme arrives at bar 47. Lyrical in concept, it contrasts with earlier music but also echoes previous motives and looks forward to the upcoming Trio theme.

Example 3.15: *Centennial (Ceremonial) March*, bars 47–58 (theme two)

As has been observed before in Willan's marches, the first strain is completed by a rescored and slightly extended repeat of theme one.

Like Elgar's march, there is no actual second strain. Instead, the music moves directly into the Trio, where a grand ceremonial melody incorporates all the patriotic fervour that might be expected of a work written for this purpose. At this point, one might anticipate balanced phrases. Willan's melody is twenty bars long and divided into two phrases of nine and eleven bars. It is perhaps a tribute to his compositional skill that the ear accepts these deviations from the perceived norm without difficulty.

Example 3.16: *Centennial (Ceremonial) March*, bars 74–93 (ceremonial theme)

The Trio is comprised of four statements of the theme in a gradually accumulating texture that climaxes at the final iteration in a rousing declaration performed by the full ensemble. As is common in British marches and as seen earlier in Willan's works, the Trio is followed by a *Da capo* repeat of initial material. Willan altered this practice slightly, beginning his repeat with the first theme and leaving out the introduction. Most ceremonial marches in English style are concluded by an extensive Coda using the Trio theme at a slower (and grander) tempo. Willan's march follows these procedures, presenting two culminating statements of his ceremonial theme, then, as he had in his *Coronation March* and as Elgar had done in *Pomp and Circumstance March No. 1*, abruptly returning to the initial tempo and first strain material to drive the music to an exuberant close.

The Canadian centennial probably did not mean much to Willan, but he apparently thought well of his *Centennial (Ceremonial) March*, commenting that it had "a couple of very pretty tunes" (Clarke 1983, 64, 114). While clearly hearkening back to similar English grand marches and to Willan's own earlier works for British royalty, it served its original patriotic purpose very well by presenting rousing, affecting, and memorable music.

Largo for Organ and Orchestra, HWC 69 (unfinished)

This score is undated and has no actual title. The designation above was added to the score by an unknown hand and is essentially a description of the work. According to Clarke, Willan began this composition in 1933 as a memorial to the Canadian organist Lynnwood Farnam,[12] but stopped after fifty-three bars and instead recast the music as a work for organ alone. The organ version was published under the title *Elegy* in 1949[13] (Clarke 1983, 185), but the autograph manuscript carries the inscription "for Organ & Orchestra" in the composer's hand, and a completion date of July 20, 1933 (Bryant 1972, 41).

The orchestral score is "clean," with no revisions or erasures, which suggests that it was copied from a previous working draft. One wonders if Clarke's chronology is incorrect, that Willan wrote the organ version first, and used that version as the basis of his orchestral scoring. The organ is not a solo instrument in the orchestral edition but is integrated into the overall sonority, often doubling either winds or strings but also adding contrapuntal lines and harmonies not in other parts.

The score as it exists is essentially two statements of an extended theme and displays several interesting compositional ideas. A short introduction (six bars) begins with a brief canon between low strings and high strings that Willan would duplicate in the first movement of Symphony No. 2.[14]

Example 3.17: *Largo*, bars 1–2

Although the key signature indicates D major,[15] this introduction is modal, circulating around three chords; E minor seventh–D major seventh–F-sharp minor. Willan sets up an interesting timbral contrast among strings, organ, and woodwinds, including an appealing echo by muted strings of a woodwind chordal passage. The theme arrives in bar seven, signalled by the first clear cadence in D major, although the tonality promptly begins wandering. Scored for cellos, it is twenty bars long with phrases of four, four, four, and eight bars. Willan enlivens the accompaniment by extracting motives from the theme and developing them imitatively.

Example 3.18: *Largo*, bars 7–26

The theme is repeated beginning at bar 28, but this time is heavily scored in flutes, clarinets, and all the strings except double basses. The accompaniment is recomposed and thickened, incorporating the brass instruments to a larger extent. Willan extends the theme by a few bars, reaching a climax that features the entire brass section, doubling and adding to the string textures. The orchestral score ends at this point, only nine bars from the end of the work, as indicated by the completed organ edition.

One cannot but wonder about the genesis of this version of the work. Orchestral compositions that include organ in a non-solo capacity are uncommon and often are challenging to perform because of the venues required.[16] A performance of an orchestral composition including organ could have been a fitting memorial for Farnam, but this piece, with limited use of the organ, seems inappropriate for such an occasion.

An equally intriguing question is why this version was left unfinished so close to the end of the piece. A comparison of the orchestral score with the completed version for organ alone shows that from the point where the orchestral score ends, the textures are simplified and recall figuration from the beginning of the work that would likely have been scored in similar fashion, not requiring much additional effort. Presumably, a particular circumstance arose where a performance of a composition for orchestra with organ was possible but fell through before Willan could complete the work, and it was set aside for consideration at a later time. Based on what survives, the composer had in this piece an interesting and practicable short contribution to the limited repertoire for orchestra with organ that, when completed, would almost certainly have attracted the interest of many conductors.

4
Works for Piano and Orchestra

Prior to leaving England for Canada, Willan started at least three works for piano and orchestra, but all were left unfinished (Bryant 1972, 44; 1982, 6). Two of these compositions remain in little more than preparatory outlines; the third is far more developed, indicating the investment of considerable effort.

All that survives of the Pianoforte Concerto in D Minor, HWC 90, is 127 bars of the finale in a rough sketch with many corrections, crossouts, and revisions. Hints of effective development can be observed, but in its fragmentary state it is difficult to surmise what this work might have been if completed. Even less survives of the Intro[duction in A Minor], HWC 91a.[1] Only fourteen bars of a *Maestoso* beginning are extant, but this appears to have been intended as the first movement of another concerto for piano and orchestra.

Ballade, HWC 86 (unfinished)

The *Ballade* for piano and orchestra, although incomplete, is a much more substantial work. The Willan collection in the National Library of Canada holds a full score of nearly 300 bars that, despite numerous revisions and erasures, displays attractive thematic materials and interesting developmental ideas, as well as imaginative scoring.

This work was almost certainly inspired by the piano music of Brahms[2] and may have been conceived when Willan was studying piano with Evlyn Howard-Jones, a Brahms expert. Clarke claims that at this time Willan planned to become a concert pianist, specializing in Brahms, but an injury to his right elbow limited his abilities and altered the direction of his career (Clarke 1986, 9). Perhaps he intended this work for performance by himself or by his teacher.

Ballade begins with a *Lento* introduction of thirty bars, similar to other orchestral compositions of this period. The connection to Brahms is immediately apparent in the opening figure, which sounds like a horn call, reminiscent of the beginnings of a number of Brahms's works.

Example 4.1: *Ballade*, bars 1–2

Willan spins the horn call into a short melody, from which he employs the opening motive in imitative development as the primary feature of the introduction.

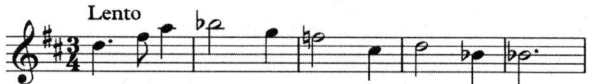

Example 4.2: *Ballade*, bars 16–20

The flattened-sixth degree that is characteristic of this motive originated in the first piano entry at bar seven. The chord progression at this point is: D major–B-flat major with added flat sixth–A dominant seventh.[3] Short motives involving rising or falling half-steps appear frequently all through this work.

The introduction is concluded by the piano alone playing a passage in parallel sixth chords (a sonority particularly favoured by Willan) that connects the introduction to the A section and will recur regularly at important points in the form.

The "A" section arrives at bar 31. Marked *Allegro* and securely in D major for the first time since the opening bars, this section presents the

Example 4.3: *Ballade*, bars 28–31

first extended theme of the work, played by clarinet over a simple tremolo chordal accompaniment in the strings. While new, this melody is clearly related to earlier material, incorporating the horn call (bars 1–4) and the motive that was extensively developed through the introduction (bar 5).

Example 4.4: *Ballade*, bars 35–42

One might expect this theme to be repeated; however, Willan instead repeats part of the parallel-sixth chord connecting passage in order to initiate a development of its third bar. The development is antiphonally conceived with the strings and piano alternating on one-bar segments. The composer extends the development by promptly repeating it with the call-and-response segments in reversed timbre. At this point, the expected repeat of theme one arrives in first violins. This initiates another extensive imitative (sometimes canonic and/or antiphonal) development using primarily the fifth bar of the theme, which is, of course, the same motive developed in the introduction. At bar 66, an interesting three-against-two hemiola is set up between the melody and accompaniment, perhaps another influence of Brahms. The A section gradually simplifies to sustained chords in strings and a piano filigree to prepare for the "B" section.

The B section, which arrives at bar 104, is at a slower tempo (*Meno mosso*) and presents a new theme in the piano that includes motives similar to earlier music.

As he had done in the A section, Willan immediately launches antiphonal development, in this instance three-part antiphony between woodwinds, strings, and piano, creating interesting timbral variety.

Meno Mosso
Cantabile

Example 4.5: *Ballade*, bars 104–11

After sixteen bars, theme two is repeated, leading to another extensive development that culminates in a climactic canonic passage. The B section is completed in an unusual way. The clarinet melody from the A section is restated, then leads into the parallel-sixth chord connecting passage that makes the transition to a new section.

The "C" section, beginning at bar 186, is again slower (*Lento*) and is in B-flat major. Willan created another new, but related, theme presented as a fourteen-bar horn melody[4] accompanied by sustained chords in the strings.

Lento, molto espressivo

Example 4.6: *Ballade*, bars 186–99

Unlike in earlier sections, this theme is immediately repeated. The first violins present the melody in octaves supported by a shimmering woodwind accompaniment. A brief piano episode connects this theme to another new melody, theme three$_1$.

Example 4.7: *Ballade*, bars 219–22

The development that follows involves a solo piano episode as well as canonic statements of theme three$_1$ and the horn theme in inversion.

At this point the score becomes very sketchy but does show some additional intriguing ideas. For example, at bar 249 the horn plays the clarinet theme—theme one from the A section—while the violins simultaneously present the horn theme—theme one from section B. Normally, these two sections would be expected to contrast with each other, but, as noted, all the themes in this work use similar motives, making this kind of integration possible. The final few bars of the score indicate that Willan intended to add another fast section, but only a few bars are sketched out.

As can be seen, *Ballade* has a number of attractive tunes and displays a considerable amount of imaginative development. Willan's use of antiphony and solo textures is also effective. While the piece is rather rigidly sectionalized, the integration of thematic material allows the sections to flow into each other without radically disturbing the overall musical shape. On the other hand, the piano writing seems rather rudimentary for a concerted work, and the (♩. ♪♩) rhythm is substantially overused. The score is undated, but this would seem to be a very early work when the composer had many interesting ideas but perhaps lacked the skill and experience to realize them in an entirely satisfactory manner.

Piano Concerto in C Minor, HWC 76

Willan's only completed concerto, the Piano Concerto in C Minor, is one of his masterpieces and among the most important Canadian works in any genre. It was written in 1944 for Agnes Butcher, whom Willan had met as a scholarship student at the Toronto Conservatory and considered a close friend (Clarke 1983, 40). Butcher had lived in Hungary for several years in the 1930s working with Béla Bartók. She returned to Canada in 1940, became a strong proponent of Bartók's piano music, and developed an international performing career. She premiered Willan's Piano Concerto in a broadcast on August 24, 1944, from the CBC Montreal studios, accompanied by the CBC Montreal Orchestra, conducted by Jean-Marie Beaudet (Bryant 1972, 76–77), and in concert on November 28 with the Toronto Symphony under Ettore Mazzoleni. Four months later, she returned to the CBC studios in Montreal to record the work with the CBC Orchestra and Beaudet (Clarke 1983, 40). In the years since these premieres the work has been recorded several times and has been played across Canada and abroad.

A large-scale composition, the concerto consists of three movements linked by interludes that create a unified, continuous whole of more than twenty-five minutes in length. Linking together the movements of large-scale compositions was not new in 1944. Franz Liszt, for example, had employed this structure in both of his piano concertos and in the Sonata in B Minor. In Liszt's case the notion of continuously unfolding form was particularly well suited to his concept of "thematic transformation" in which all the themes throughout the work were related but varied to provide contrast. Some scholars consider Liszt's transformation of themes to be among his most important contributions to musical composition and have noted its similarity to twentieth-century serialism (Searle 1980, 61).

Binding the movements together may be even more appropriate for Willan's concerto. Themes and thematic elements are liberally repeated throughout all movements verbatim or in various aurally identifiable modifications, making this music so tightly integrated that the bridging of the movements becomes almost a requirement of the overall form. Clarke observes that since Willan, in both the first and third movement of this work, does not return to the tonic key until the final bars, the indivisibility of the work is essential (Clarke 1983, 103).

The first and third movements of Willan's Piano Concerto in C Minor are in an individualized version of sonata-allegro form, in which Willan's harmonic usage renders the usual tonal relationships irrelevant. In his concept of sonata-allegro form, thematic materials and tempo changes define formal divisions, since the fluidity of the key areas undermines the identification of structural components according to tonal centres. When approaching his music, as with many other twentieth-century composers, identifying primary and secondary *areas*, rather than themes, makes for more revealing analyses.

The first movement opens with a piano flourish following a two-bar timpani roll supported by tremolo low strings. The flourish presents the first primary theme (P1), of which the opening motive, three descending semi-tones, will become a significant constituent in a number of thematic elements throughout the entire work and, as such, a highly significant unifying factor.[5]

Example 4.8: Piano Concerto in C Minor, bars 3–9 (P1)

Willan promptly repeats a condensed version of the piano flourish that leads to the beginning of the primary area proper at bar 20. The main theme here, in piano, is a derivation of P1. Curiously, it carries the notation (♩ = 72), which suggests a slower tempo than the preceding *Allegro energico*, despite the close relationship between the two versions of P1. At this point, another important motive appears in violas that is a development of the semitone motive from the first bars and will recur in several adaptations as the movement progresses.

Example 4.9: Piano Concerto in C Minor, bars 21–23 (P2)

For the next thirty-five bars, Willan develops P1 and P2. The music assigned to the piano draws mostly on P1, while the orchestra generally focuses on P2, especially the semitone motive, or contributes new material. Another motive that will also have later significance, particularly in the interludes between movements, emerges at bar 55.

Fifteen bars later (bar 70), the horns present a distinctive melodic fragment that will become a major unifying element not only of the first movement, but of the work as a whole. While this fragment, with its distinctive three descending semitones, was suggested in the piano from

Example 4.10: Piano Concerto in C Minor, 55–61 (P3)

the opening bars and is similar to P2, it will recur throughout the concerto in various guises and scorings, although it is primarily associated with the horns, ensuring that it will be heard on all of its appearances and providing both melodic and timbral unity.

Example 4.11: Piano Concerto in C Minor, bars 70–72 (P4)

Willan repeats it three times to ensure its easy recognition, then recalls part of P3 to prepare for an upcoming surprise.

An abrupt change of tempo and, to some degree, material arrives at bar 80. The metre is altered from 3/4 to *Alla breve* with a tempo marking of *Allegro* (♩ = 118), essentially tripling the tempo. This segment skilfully transitions from the primary to the secondary area of the formal scheme. The material is drawn from P1, but the piano develops this theme into octave passagework, which will be a feature of the secondary area. Short, descending half-step figures are also incorporated.

The secondary area enters at bar 99. In contrast to the rather rhapsodic music of the primary area (Clarke 1983, 103), the music here is agitated and dominated by octave passagework in the piano, plus pedal seventh chords and a considerable amount of development of half-step contrary motion. The initial motive (S1), played twice, appears in solo trumpet answered by woodwinds, in call-and-response texture. Set against quiet, sustained pedal chords and the piano octaves, the wind timbres are striking and firmly establish S1 in the listener's ear in preparation for its reappearance throughout the development—an astute scoring decision on Willan's part.

Example 4.12: Piano Concerto in C Minor, bars 101–5 (S1)

In a work that is so thematically unified, it probably comes as no surprise that the second melodic element of the secondary area is another incarnation of P1 (including a quotation of its opening notes in augmentation in solo clarinet), giving the Exposition as a whole a hint of monothematicism and an allusion to sonata-rondo form. However, Willan's Exposition is not yet complete. The concluding motive of the secondary area is a figure that occurs frequently in several slightly adapted forms in this concerto and in both of Willan's symphonies. Clarke has named it the "Willan motto" (Clarke 1983, 94). The concluding bars of the Exposition consist of an antiphonal development of this motive.

Example 4.13: Piano Concerto in C Minor, bars 140–43 ("Willan motto")

The Development probably begins at bar 148, but a considerable amount of development has already occurred. The first section draws on S1 and the Willan motto, but continuing short chromatic lines also recall primary area material. A new theme is introduced at bar 173, marked *Poco meno mosso—cantabile*.[6] While not specifically related to previous material, this theme includes motives that have been heard as early as bar 36 in the melody or in accompanying contrapuntal strands, allowing it to evolve comfortably out of previous material.

Willan states this theme only once before proceeding to an imitative development of the Willan motto, which leads into the cadenza. As expected, the cadenza is virtuosic and is based on three thematic elements: P4, the development theme, and the Willan motto. Following this section, a short transition is inserted before the Recapitulation that does

Example 4.14: Piano Concerto in C Minor, bar 173–81

not seem to be specifically related to earlier music, although a fragment of P4 appears in the final bars.

Only a fraction of the Exposition is recapitulated and only elements related to P1. In fact, the Recapitulation (bars 219–50) might better be considered secondary development of the primary theme; however, the return of P1 and the tonic key does provide a feeling of recapitulation. During this section, the piano contributes momentum through octave passagework, broken octaves, and a series of right-hand arpeggios over left-hand alternating C minor and B-flat major descending chords that stride down the keyboard and drive the music forward to culminate on a C major chord in bar 247. The piano leads into interlude one, connecting movement one to movement two.

The principal elements of interlude 1 are P3 and P4, although other fragments of primary material are also present. A short flute solo over P3 foreshadows the first theme of the upcoming second movement, an effective means of making this material refer both backward and forward.

Example 4.15: Piano Concerto in C Minor, bars 270–74

The second movement (*Adagio*) arrives at bar 277 and is structured in ternary form. A simple accompaniment in the strings and rippling arpeggios in solo piano support the theme of the A section, a haunting English horn solo. The presentation of this theme is completed by the bassoon, emerging out of the tone of the English horn—a novel and ingenious timbral variation.

Example 4.16: Piano Concerto in C Minor, bars 280–93

The effect is delightful. The listener hears a change of colour, but since both instruments are double reeds with similar timbre, the melody holds together and the change of instrument allows it to be completed without the ending being heard as a separate element. The insight displayed in this small touch is apparent when one realizes that no change of timbre was necessary: these final pitches of the tune are easily within the compass of the English horn. The instrument exchange could only have been undertaken with the intention of creating a subtle alteration in the instrumental colour that emphasizes both the similarity of, and the difference between, the instrumental timbres.[7]

A "quasi cadenza" for the soloist follows the presentation of the theme. The accompanimental arpeggios that have persisted through the movement to this point evolve into cascading diminished seventh chords and ultimately into a partial statement of the English horn theme that provides a link to the B section.

The B section is short (twelve bars) and its theme is a lyrical, three-bar motive initially presented by strings and woodwinds, then taken up by piano.

Example 4.17: Piano Concerto in C Minor, bars 312–14

The return of the cascading diminished seventh chords and tremolo strings completes this section.

The transition back to the A section is complex. Willan inserts a segment based on P4 from the first movement that actually appears (in horns and trombones) before the completion of the B section. Recalling this motive reinforces the cyclic nature of the thematic material in this work but is an unusual addition to ternary form. When presented antiphonally by horns and piano with very little accompaniment, it firmly establishes an aural link with the previous movement and primes the listener for its reappearance in subsequent music. A chromatic rising sequence in piano prepares for a culminating statement of the theme of the B section, powerfully scored for the full brass section in chorale-like texture.

Example 4.18: Piano Concerto in C Minor, bars 333–35

Brass chorales as structural articulations have been noted earlier in this study and will be seen again in both of Willan's symphonies. Placed where it is in the form, this chorale functions as both a dramatic climax to the B section and a clear auditory separation of the two primary sections of the form. A brief piano development of the chorale completes the transition.

The A section returns at bar 341 to fulfill the constituents of ternary form. It consists of a rapturous full-orchestra restatement of the initial theme of the movement, after which the texture recedes in preparation for interlude two, the link between movements two and three. During the textural recession, Willan inserts a reminiscence of P3 from movement one, thereby establishing the first of several connections between the two interludes.

Another extraordinary orchestrational idea occurs during this recall of the main theme. With the exception of one small-scale composition that will be addressed later in this book, Willan's music does not include substantial use of percussion. His orchestral and wind band music generally employs only timpani in both traditional and distinctive roles. From the traditional perspective, the timpani are often coupled with the brass instruments and support crescendos and climaxes, emphasize important rhythms, add rhythmic momentum, and contribute to drama or mood. Many examples of such functions can be found throughout these scores.

However, Willan's timpani parts sometimes show distinctive approaches. As noted frequently in this book, he was fond of beginning works with timpani rolls, most of which start from virtual silence and crescendo to significant volume before the entry of other instruments. Examples are not difficult to find—*Coronation March*, *Royal Salute*, and *Centennial March* fit this pattern, and, indeed, the Piano Concerto in C Minor almost does as well. He also occasionally writes more complex timpani parts that simplify important melodic or contrapuntal ideas. A quite astonishing timpani part appears in the counterpoint to the euphoric restatement of the main theme, where the timpani play an altered version of the bass line.

Example 4.19: Piano Concerto in C Minor, bars 345–46

Interlude two, which arrives at bar 362, consists of essentially the same material as interlude one. Willan reduced the scoring to a trio—flute, cello, and piano. Cello and flute respond to each other while the piano fills in the harmony and adds rhythmic momentum. Since both interludes have flute solos, a timbral association is apparent, but the flute solo here also recalls motivic material from the earlier interlude. The cello part is essentially a continuous development of P4, which, of course, was also an essential element of interlude one.

Example 4.20: Piano Concerto in C Minor, bars 362–70

However, as he had accomplished in the previous interlude, Willan makes this music look forward as well. The Trio dissolves into a piano passage that quotes directly from the primary theme of the imminent third movement.

The third movement (*Allegro con spirito*) is cast in a version of sonata-allegro form similar to the first movement, but is complicated by the recall of earlier material. The primary theme (1P)[8] has its roots in Willan's early, unfinished Piano Concerto in D Minor but was substantially recomposed for its use here (Clarke 1983, 104).

Willan states it three times in succession: by the orchestra in E-flat major, by the piano in D major, and by both orchestra and piano in E-flat major with virtuosic figuration in the piano. His harmonic usage is more diatonic than at any other point in this piece, but is not strictly functional. The composer's interest in unusual phrasing persists here; the melody appears to be phrased in four, five, and seven bars, although the harmony does not always support the cadences, opening the possibility of longer groupings. Consisting of a number of discrete motives, the

Example 4.21: Piano Concerto in C Minor, bars 387–402 (1P)

theme offered Willan excellent potential for development, as will be seen. These three statements of the melody encompass the entire primary area.

The secondary area commences at bar 438 with no preceding transition. In contrast to the primary area, melodic material consists of three motives of varying lengths.[9] Secondary areas based on melodic fragments instead of fully developed melodies were also not new in 1944; they date back at least to Beethoven's Symphony No. 3.

The first secondary motive, which appears immediately, is the Willan motto extended by several bars.

Example 4.22: Piano Concerto in C Minor, bars 438–42 (1S)

The composer makes no further use of this motive; however, it helps to connect this movement with earlier music. Harmonized more or less diatonically in B major, it creates an abrupt contrast with the preceding music in E-flat major.

The next motive (2S) is very brief and might be considered simply a connecting idea except for its extensive role in both Exposition and Development.

The longest of the secondary motives, 3S is related to two previous themes. Its first three notes are drawn from the B section theme of movement two, and a distinctive minor seventh skip relates it to P1 of

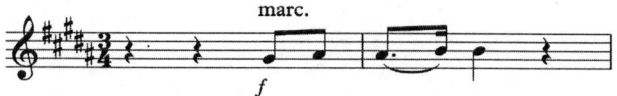

Example 4.23: Piano Concerto in C Minor, bars 442–43 (2S)

the first movement. This secondary motive also will be very significant in the evolution of the third movement.

Example 4.24: Piano Concerto in C Minor, bars 449–57 (3S)

While 3S is being presented, the woodwinds engage in an imitative development of 2S, and, following its completion, both brass and woodwinds present a rhythmically simplified version of P4 from movement one, a primary integrating element of the work as a whole.

At bar 462, the piano introduces a new melody that begins as a sequential presentation of bars 2 and 3 of 1P and then develops in a new direction to be followed by a brief canon based on bar 2 of the same theme. These references to the primary area give the Exposition a structure similar to movement one by hinting at sonata-rondo form.

The Development arrives at bar 482. The first subsection (bars 482–94) essentially follows expected procedures with an antiphonal development (horns and violins) of the first motive of 3S, and a hint of 2S in imitation in woodwinds. However, at this point (bar 495) Willan does something completely unexpected. Instead of applying the usual techniques of symphonic development to his thematic material, he simply restates the entire final section of the Exposition starting with the presentation of the last half of 3S, and the recall of the derived versions of 1P. The final part of 3S is altered only in scoring; the recall of 1P is transposed up a full tone. Simply repeating material from the Exposition as part of the Development is certainly an atypical procedure that may be unique to this work.

Another unusual idea, but not surprising in the context of this work, is a recall of P4 from movement one, confirming the cyclic aspect of thematic material. The opening four notes of this motive appear in unaccompanied trombones in bar 516, are promptly combined with 2S, and developed for the next twelve bars.

At this point, Willan introduces a harmonic "stroke of genius" (Clarke 1983, 105). A piano passage is inserted that constitutes a ten-bar prolongation of a third-inversion dominant-seventh chord on G. As Clarke observes, this leads listeners to expect a cadence in C major, but instead the composer presents 1P in B major—a truly thrilling musical event. 1P is stated in its entirety and might be considered the Recapitulation except for the additional intriguing development that follows. Willan provides a distinctive development of 2S in three-part antiphony (woodwinds, piano, strings) that is promptly restated and somewhat expanded. Since the texture presented here is rare in this work, these bars stand out aurally and signal the beginning of a four-part structural articulation leading to the Recapitulation.

Example 4.25: Piano Concerto in C Minor, bars 565–69

To reinforce the transition into the Recapitulation Willan adds several striking events to the structural articulation: a cadenza-like bar in the piano that recalls the P1 from the very beginning of the concerto; an accompanied reminiscence of the prolonged dominant-seventh chord on G from earlier in the Development, itself a smaller structural articulation; and a low-brass chorale similar to that which appeared at the same point in movement two, and in other orchestral works at significant locations in the form.

The Recapitulation probably begins at bar 589. The primary theme of the movement (1P) arrives in C major, not the original key of this movement, but the first time the tonality of the work as a whole has been established since the first movement (Clarke 1983, 105). The marking *Nobilmente* that appears here suggests a slower tempo; however, a few bars later Willan will introduce a long *Allargando*, which probably renders a slower tempo impractical at this point. Like movement one, the Recapitulation is truncated and employs mostly primary material. A brief reference to the Willan motto appears at bars 612–13, and a descending chromatic line that seems to recall movement two (see Example 4.19) occurs two bars later. At the climax of this section, horns and trombones present an augmented version of the first phrase of 3S.

Example 4.26: Piano Concerto in C Minor, bars 616–22

In the context of the continually slowing tempo and the brass instrument scoring, these bars are very dramatic. Motives related to primary material in full orchestra scoring and virtuosic passagework in the piano bring the work to a powerful close.

Willan's Piano Concerto in C Minor is widely accepted as one of his most successful and influential works. Undoubtedly, its tight organization around a limited number of distinctive motives and its overall lyricism are major factors in arriving at this assessment. When Willan undertook this composition he was in the midst of two other major works, Symphony No. 2 and the opera *Deirdre*. He is quoted as saying: "I had written part of my second Symphony; I broke off to write the music for *Deirdre*, and stopped half-way through the second act in order to write a piano concerto; I then returned to *Deirdre*, finished it, and then I completed my symphony" (Clarke 1983, 126).

Willan apparently always wanted to write a piano concerto, and when the opportunity arose he seized it, even though it meant postponing work on other major projects. In many ways the pleasure he felt in writing the Piano Concerto in C Minor, for a friend and with virtually an assurance of performance, can be sensed in this music. He said he deliberately "filled it full of tunes" (Clarke 1983, 106), an indication of his enjoyment in creating it. The work continues to reward listeners and performers alike.

5

The Symphonies

Willan came late to the composition of symphonies. When his first symphony appeared in 1936, he was almost fifty-six years old and was well established in other genres. Clarke suggests that he, like Brahms, was in "awe of the symphonic form and the composer's responsibility in regard to it, and he did not want to rush the composition of his symphonies without adequate reflection" (Clarke 1983, 95). While this may be true, Willan had, as already seen earlier in this study, a long-standing interest in orchestral music dating back at least to 1904. His situation in Canada may have had more impact on any decision to engage in large-scale orchestral works than any personal trepidation about the form. While a considerable amount of quality orchestral playing had occurred in Canada prior to the First World War, most of the orchestras disbanded during the war and their re-establishment afterwards took considerable time. Only after about 1930 were concert orchestras operating on any kind of professional basis again in the country (Kallmann 1960, 270). In this context, there was little incentive until the 1930s for Willan to engage in orchestral composition of any kind, let alone to create symphonies.

Willan's symphonies were not the first written by a Canadian composer, but they are probably the first symphonies written *in* Canada. Calixa Lavallée[1] apparently composed a choral symphony in the 1880s, which was written in, and dedicated to, the city of Boston. The score is lost (Potvin 1992, 728). Percival Price's[2] symphony *The St. Lawrence* had two performances in Toronto in 1934, but was composed in Vienna (Barnwell 1992, 1076). Clarence Lucas[3] also wrote a symphony, but spent a small part of his professional life in Canada, living at various times in New York, London, and Paris, although he was remembered in Canada as the country's most versatile composer (Kallmann 1960, 253, 255). It is highly unlikely that any part of his symphony was written in Canada.

Symphony No. 1 in D Minor, HWC 70

Willan's first symphony was completed in full score on September 15, 1936 (Bryant 1972, 41) but in some ways had been in gestation since before 1910. A considerable amount of the thematic material was drawn from Willan's early orchestral works, finished and unfinished. It was premiered quickly. Reginald Stewart conducted the first and third performances with the Toronto Promenade Symphony Orchestra on October 8, 1936, and July 1, 1937[4] (Clarke 1983, 31, 33). Douglas Clarke conducted the second performance on February 14, 1937, with the Montreal Symphony (Clarke 1983, 32).[5] In the years between 1936 and 1949 the work received seven performances in Toronto and Montreal, including two of the second movement alone,[6] but since 1949 it has rarely appeared in concert, probably because Willan's Symphony No. 2, which was premiered in 1950, has tended to overshadow its predecessor. The first symphony is in three movements, without a Scherzo.

Like a number of works already reviewed, the first movement begins with a timpani roll and a *Largo* introduction. The main theme of the Introduction (I1), presented by low strings, sets an appropriately serious mood and will be the source of thematic motives throughout the movement.

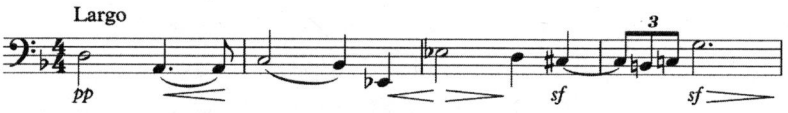

Example 5.1: Symphony No. 1, first movement, bars 2–5 (I1)

In bar 7, a syncopated rhythm and an accented weak beat may be intended to prepare the extensive use of hemiola employed in the movement.

Most of the Introduction is a development of the first bars of I1, often accompanied by a chromatic line in coupled thirds. Similar

Example 5.2: Symphony No. 1, first movement, bar 7

motives and accompaniments will have prominent roles in upcoming music.

Willan concludes the thirty-bar Introduction with a short chorale that appears first in woodwinds, then in brass, and ultimately is completed by a solo timpani roll, ending this section as it began. This chorale has structural significance at many points in the movement and, indeed, in the work as a whole. As previously observed, brass chorales as structural articulations are Willan fingerprints in his large orchestral works.

Example 5.3: Symphony No. 1, first movement, bars 26–30

The primary area (*Allegro feroce*) of the sonata-allegro form commences at bar 31. The first theme (P1) was drawn from the orchestral rhapsody *From the Highlands* of 1911 and is developed to substantial length in both the Exposition and Development of this movement.

Example 5.4: Symphony No. 1, first movement, bars 31–34 (P1)

Willan repeats it three times in accumulating texture and with progressively longer and more complex extensions between the repeats. During the second extension, he develops the hemiola figures that are a major feature of the development of primary area themes.

Example 5.5: Symphony No. 1, first movement, bars 54–55

This extension also introduces a fanfare-like motive (P2) that the composer will use to connect passages and to enliven heavily scored, or rhythmically slow-moving, blocks of sound.

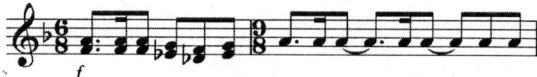

Example 5.6: Symphony No. 1, first movement, bars 66–67 (P2—winds)

The third statement of P1 (bars 68–71) is climactic, after which a quick textural recession leads to a recall of the woodwind and brass chorales from the end of the Introduction, signalling the beginning of what is, in effect, a development of primary material within the Exposition. Developmental episodes within the expositions of sonata form movements were common in the nineteenth and early twentieth centuries, but Willan here extended the practice beyond what might usually be expected. Willan's developmental episode employs motives from both P1 and P2 and features sequential passages, often in hemiola, as well as imitation.

This energetic episode comes to an abrupt end at bar 114 as the busy texture is suddenly reduced to a single horn note that becomes a pedal over which woodwinds and strings present the now-familiar chorale from the closing bars of the Introduction. Since the counterpoint, texture, and harmonic rhythm abruptly are simplified, one might expect a slower tempo as well. Willan prevents any reduction of momentum by inserting a phrase from P1 in cellos and bassoons.

The transition to the secondary area begins at bar 126. The timbre, woodwinds and strings, connects these measures to the preceding chorale, but the transitional music is chordal, created through stepwise contrary movement in all voices. The secondary key, which also appears at this point, is a surprising E major, far removed from the primary key (D minor), although composers like Stravinsky had begun contrasting second-related keys in sonata-form movements early in the twentieth century.[7] Since the secondary area will be at a slower tempo, a gradual *ritardando* through the transitional section would be appropriate.

The secondary area begins at bar 138 in 3/4 time and marked *Andante cantabile*. The lyrical theme (S1) in first violins is supported by an accomplished contrapuntal accompaniment firmly in E major.

Example 5.7: Symphony No. 1, first movement, bars 138–47 (S1)

As he had done in the primary area, Willan repeats his theme three times in accumulating texture. At the third statement the key signature is changed to C major, but the tonality wanders freely, and the melody is entrusted to violas, cellos, English horn, clarinet, and low horns, creating a pleasing textural inversion. While this statement is somewhat extended, Willan does not launch a development of secondary themes as he had in the primary area. During the concluding bars of the third statement of S1, motives from P1 begin to appear in the counterpoint.

Willan also inserts a four-bar phrase that is clearly derived from I1 but will recur very prominently later in the movement and is here labelled S2 in acknowledgement of its importance. Scored for clarinet and bassoon with spare accompaniment, it is easily heard and remembered even though it is stated only once.

Example 5.8: Symphony No. 1, first movement, bars 171–74 (S2)

Following S2, Willan begins a transition to the Development. The motives from P1 heard earlier are repeated along with lyrical woodwind solo lines and phrases in the strings that recall the chorale from the end of the Introduction. P2 is also present, adding momentum to these passages.

The Development, which begins at bar 188, is almost entirely concerned with primary material, but also includes a few new motives that relate aurally to earlier material. Textures are frequently imitative, including *fugato*, and, not surprisingly, include considerable use of hemiola. Particularly dramatic moments occur at bar 212, where the horns powerfully extend P2 for eight bars while unison strings present the melody of the woodwind–brass chorale from the Introduction, and at bar 246 and 248, where horns and trombones forcefully enunciate an augmentation of the first bar of P1.

Development comes to a sudden halt on the first beat of bar 270. After a silent fermata, Willan inserts a completely unexpected *Largo* section based on S2. The composer himself explained this curious addition as a codetta appearing at the end of the Development instead of at the end of the Exposition where it might have been anticipated (Clarke 1983, 93); however, one wonders if instead he felt the need to add some secondary material to the Development in light of the fact that to this point it had been virtually exclusively concerned with primary material, and he was about to return again to the primary area in the Recapitulation. On the other hand, the tempo is that of the Introduction not the

Example 5.9: Symphony No. 1, first movement, bars 212–19

Example 5.10: Symphony No. 1, first movement, bars 246–48

secondary area, although S2, as noted earlier, was derived from the main melody (I1) of the Introduction. The connection to the Introduction is further reinforced by the return of the chromatic, coupled-third accompaniment that supported earlier derivations of this theme. Clarke believes that Willan erred in adding this segment at this point in the movement, since it robs the music of its energy and excitement (Clarke 1983, 93). While the drive to the Recapitulation is certainly suspended, this insert does provide variety to a long section that has largely been monothematically constructed. Perhaps the effect would be less unsettling if the tempo were *Andante cantabile*, the pace of the secondary area, instead of the Introduction. Interestingly, the Development ends with another timpani solo, a rewarding touch of musical integration.

The Recapitulation, arriving at bar 294, is virtually identical to the Exposition with the expected changes of pitch level and orchestration, as well as a few truncations or extensions of certain passages. The only surprise occurs at the Coda, where Willan repeats the *Largo* from the end of the Development and extends it to accomplish a quiet closing. The final bars offer a remarkable orchestrational idea. The final D-minor chord is sustained for two bars, but in the final bar all instruments are withdrawn except two horns, trombones, and tuba, a timbre reminiscent of the end of the Introduction, and perhaps a continuation of a previously noted structural principle—sustained brass sound preparing the listener for a new event, in this case, the second movement. It is also a reminder that Willan was an organist. The timbre change sounds very much like an organist varying registrations on sustained chords to add aural interest, especially on final sonorities.

The Adagio has been described by Clarke as "rhapsodic," a word chosen to illustrate not only the mood, but also the harmony, which explores a wide range of tonal areas and incorporates much chromatic voice leading. The form is also difficult to specify precisely (Clarke 1983, 93), although three themes and two motivic elements can be identified and are the basis of development through the movement. The music seems to have been originally composed for this movement, with the exception of theme one (identified below), which first appeared in 1912 in Willan's song *Dreams*. Although it adheres to no identifiable form, the overall structure is tightly organized around the development of a few melodic ideas, allowing it to be successfully performed as an independent piece (Clarke 1983, 93).

The dreamy Introduction presents the two motivic ideas that will be building blocks for the upcoming music. The first appears immediately in the strings and comprises an exotic-sounding descending diminished-fourth chord progression[8] that will recur in original and adapted form.

The second motive is presented a few bars later by the clarinets, surprisingly, in coupled perfect fourths. Willan will use this music to connect episodes of thematic development and also as melodic accompaniment.

Solo horn presents theme one over a simple, almost diatonic, B-flat major accompaniment in strings.

A restatement of motive 1 in an altered version connects to a melodic and rhythmic development of theme one by solo oboe and solo flute, over a shimmering string accompaniment.

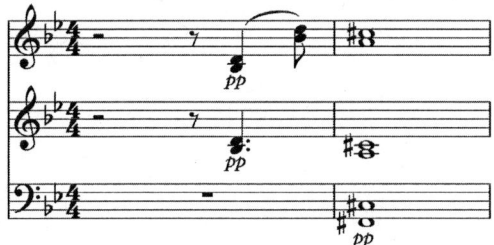

Example 5.11: Symphony No. 1, second movement, bars 1–2 (motive 1)

Example 5.12: Symphony No. 1, second movement, bars 6–10 (motive 2)

Example 5.13: Symphony No. 1, second movement, bars 11-15 (theme one)

Example 5.14: Symphony No. 1, second movement, bars 17–20 (solo oboe)

Beginning at bar 27, the key signature changes frequently, but the harmony does not necessarily conform to the key. Throughout this rather long section, Willan employs motive 2 expanded to closed-position seventh chords almost continuously, linking segments together and providing accompaniment for two new themes.

Theme two, a flute solo, does not seem to be related to any previous material. It appears only twice, both times in solo flute, and does not figure prominently in the musical dialogue, although triplet passages similar to those in this theme do occur.

Theme three is the most extended melodic element in the movement and is the basis of the largest amount of development. When it arrives

Example 5.15: Symphony No. 1, second movement, bars 29–30 (theme two—flute solo)

at bar 36, Willan ensured that it would be heard by scoring it for flutes, clarinet, bassoon, first violins (in octaves), and cellos.

Example 5.16: Symphony No. 1, second movement, bars 36–41 (theme three)

A repeat of theme two with a new key signature (B major) brings this section of the movement to a close. Since the music that follows is highly developmental, these first forty-nine bars have many of the properties of an Exposition, in that they introduce the musical material of the rest of the movement without engaging in much development.

The following section, beginning at bar 51, functions as a Development. Most of the thematic elements return in various adaptions and no new material is introduced. Two subsections are apparent. The first of these focuses on theme three and sets bars 1 and 2 against bars 3 and 4 in counterpoint. Ten bars long, it comes to a gentle close on three quiet chords under fermatas that produce a clear cadence in D major. The second subsection commences at bar 62 and is considerably longer, gradually building to a massive climax at bar 103. It starts by recalling the textures of the very beginning of the movement. Motive 1 appears twice in adapted versions, and the first four bars of theme three, somewhat elongated, are also present, as is a reference to motive 2. Theme one returns in a glorious full orchestra setting at bar 76 and is followed by a substantial development of its second and third bars. As the texture accumulates toward the climax, references to both motives can be easily identified, and an almost complete statement of theme three in trumpets and trombones leads into the climactic bars that culminate in a resonant cadence to the tonic, B-flat major.

During the textural recession following the climax, Willan introduces a descending three-note motive that is drawn from the surprising *Largo* that appeared at the end of the Development and in the Coda of the first movement. The connection to the first movement is further reinforced a few bars later when the music segues into the brass chorale from the Introduction (and a number of other places) in the initial movement. It functions here precisely as it has in other works, as a structural articulation preparing for the Coda, but also establishes an aspect of cyclic form within the complete symphony.

The Coda (bar 111) is remarkably tender and restrained. Shimmering strings support brief references to the beginning of theme three, and later, motive 2 enlivens a subtle repeat of bars 2 and 3 of theme one. The final bars are spectacular. Over quiet sustained chords in strings and horns, the flutes play a duet in coupled thirds comprised of a rising sequence based on the first three notes of theme one. This duet is followed by another: two solo violins develop the opening three notes of theme three in parallel fourths and rise in leisurely fashion into their high register, supported by rippling harp arpeggios. The effect seems transcendent, as if one's eyes were being drawn mystically toward the sky. Ultimately, the music simply dissolves into a reassuring silence.

This superbly constructed movement captivates listeners in an aurally engaging and emotionally moving soundscape that has also attracted conductors to this music, even when performance of the complete symphony has not been practical.

The title, *Allegro jubilante*, gives a clear indication of the exuberant, even celebratory, character of the third movement, the finale of the symphony. This movement is more complex than the previous two. Willan includes several brief thematic motives, incorporates melodies from earlier compositions, and recalls material from earlier movements of this work, securing the cyclic nature of the form. Possibly because of the plethora of thematic material, the composer also employs a unique version of sonata-allegro form. While primary and secondary areas are easily delineated, the Exposition flows into the Development with no apparent division, rendering it impossible to determine precisely where one section ends and the other begins. No separation occurs between Development and Recapitulation either, but it is not difficult to identify the return of primary material, despite the fact that Willan begins his Recapitulation partway through the Exposition, instead of at its beginning. The Coda is more than sixty bars long and begins with a sixteen-bar development of a passage from another work entirely and, at its climax, recalls theme one from the second movement. However, regardless of the diverse sources of material, the composer is able to hold the movement together quite well and bring the symphony to an exciting finish.

The energetic nature of this movement is established immediately. The first segment (ten bars) of the primary area consists of a "Willan rush," as seen in similar situations in other compositions, and introduces two short thematic motives and the first theme of the movement. A closer inspection reveals that most of these bars were taken directly from the second part (bars 32–38) of an early, unfinished orchestral work, reviewed earlier in this book under the title *Lento mistico*. The first thematic motive (1M)[9] appears in bar 4 and entails an accented arpeggiation of a diminished triad in the bass voices. This figure will recur several times and adds substantial energy to the bass line.

Example 5.17: Symphony No. 1, third movement, bar 4 (1M)

The second significant motive (2M) is a rising triplet figure in horns and trombones that bears a resemblance to the first bar of the primary theme (P1) of the first movement and begins the process of recalling thematic ideas from earlier in the symphony.

Example 5.18: Symphony No. 1, third movement, bars 6–7 (2M)

Presented simultaneously with these motives is the initial theme of the movement (1P), which, like the Willan rush, is drawn from *Lento mistico*. Clarke remarked that the second bar of this theme is related to bars 1 and 2 of the theme from the Introduction to the first movement (I1) (Clarke 1983, 93), which may be the reason Willan felt it fit well into his symphony. He extended the original melody by two bars to link to the next section of the primary area.

Example 5.19: Symphony No. 1, third movement, bars 4–8 (1P)

The next major thematic element of the movement (2P) is a dramatic unison horn call that was also taken from an early work, in this case the *Overture* (with the Whitman quotation, "Know'st thou the excellent joys of youth"). Presented over only tremolo string chords, these bars impress themselves into the listener's ear and ensure that they will be remembered.

Example 5.20: Symphony No. 1, third movement, bars 11–14 (2P)

This theme appears again at bar 21, transposed down a major third to B-flat major and scored in trombones. This appearance has special structural significance, since this is the point at which Willan will choose to begin his Recapitulation. The composer gives this initial part of the primary area a miniature a-b-a form by recalling material from the beginning. The first repeated music is 2M, this time developed sequentially between horns and trumpets, and followed by 1P and 1M delivered concurrently, as they had originally appeared.

The primary area includes another important thematic element. The Willan motto, in a somewhat extended form, is inserted and developed sequentially for the next seventeen bars.

Example 5.21: Symphony No. 1, third movement, bars 36–38 (3P)

The transition to the secondary area is interesting. It begins with another statement of 2P exactly as it had first appeared—in unison horns accompanied by tremolo strings—but transposed down a major second to C major. There follow four bars that employ another motive from *Lento mistico* (bars 54–55):

Example 5.22: Symphony No. 1, third movement, bars 57–58 (bars 54–55 of *Lento mistico*)

Clarke points out that this transition is too short to accomplish all that it must: change tempo and style from *Allegro jubilante* to *Andante cantabile*, change metre from 4/4 to 3/4, change key from D major to A major (Clarke 1983, 94). The accuracy of Clarke's observation is confirmed by the fact that conductors of this work have felt it necessary to interpolate a *ritardando molto* through these bars in order to effect a smooth connection, even though no such direction appears in the score.

The secondary area has but one theme, which is drawn from yet another early work, the *Epilogue* of 1909. Marked *Andante cantabile*, it is scored for strings and woodwinds only, a dramatic contrast from the primary area, which, with the exception of the horn call (2P), was largely scored for full orchestra. At the outset of this section, the first bassoon has a syncopated accompaniment figure that adds considerable momentum, and later, the bassoons double the contrary-motion counterpoint in the other strings, creating a much more effective accompaniment than Willan had written for this theme when it appeared in *Epilogue*.

Like Willan's earlier work, the melody is fourteen bars long and is promptly restated, although the repeat begins modulating by the fifth bar. Following the second statement of the theme, Willan engages in a substantial imitative (almost canonic) development of the eleventh bar of the theme, along with a reference to its first four bars. As noted earlier, the Exposition flows into the Development without the slightest separation.

Clarke suggests bar 111 as the beginning of the Development (Clarke 1983, 94), which seems the most logical choice since the tempo is increased to *Poco animato*, and a syncopated fragment of the horn call (2P) also appears.[10]

Example 5.23: Symphony No. 1, third movement, bars 60–73 (S)

Example 5.24: Symphony No. 1, third movement, bars 112–17

This emergence of music from the primary area is brief; Willan promptly returns to secondary material, including the motive from bar 11 of S that was earlier developed imitatively and to references to the first bars of the secondary theme, in remarkably well-designed contrapuntal textures. This subsection concludes abruptly in a brass chorale and a solo timpani roll that, as usual, signal the arrival of new material.

The second subsection of the Development is indeed new material. The key reverts to the tonic, D major, the meter to 4/4, and a considerable development of motive 1 and theme three from the second movement is commenced. Willan's counterpoint is again highly effective, and he also employs gradually increased scoring to build this subsection to a climax at bar 180, which ushers in another subsection based on elements from 1P and the Willan motto.

This third subsection of the Development is designed to generate textural variety but also maintain momentum. Willan mixes full orchestra scoring with passages featuring twisting woodwind solos, and then gathers the orchestral forces in a massive crescendo that sprints precipitously into the Recapitulation.

As noted earlier, Willan does not recapitulate the entire Exposition, but starts at bar 21—where the trombones intone 2P in B-flat major. From this point onward the primary and secondary areas follow with minor emendations; however, the Willan motto is treated in different tonalities than it was in the Exposition, and the secondary theme appears in B-flat major rather than in the expected tonic, D major. The transition also seems to work better than it did in the Exposition, probably because the C major statement of 2P is absent (Clarke 1983, 94–95).

Willan prepares the Coda in two ways. First, he inserts a short segment that is, in essence, a full orchestra fanfare. The harmonic rhythm slows down, although the actual chords are created through the contrapuntal movement of voices and become quite dissonant, and the surface rhythm is simplified to figures imitating trumpet calls. At the same time, the horns present a melody that is reminiscent, at least in mood, of the first secondary theme (S1) from the first movement.

Example 5.25: Symphony No. 1, third movement, bars 295–301

Second, Willan writes a four-bar segment that features the brass and timpani, another timbrally based structural articulation that is in keeping with his practice throughout this and other compositions. This passage, consisting of seventh chords, added-note sonorities, and augmented chords, leads the music back to D major and launches the multi-faceted and climactic Coda.

Curiously, the Coda, beginning at bar 308 at a faster tempo (*Allegro*), initially develops another motive from the early work, *Lento mistico*. Willan extracted seven bars directly from his previous composition (bars 54–60) and developed them for some twenty-six bars. The motive employed, however, is not entirely new to this work since the composer had used a two-bar fragment of it in the transition between the primary and secondary areas in both Exposition and Recapitulation. Such a substantive development of a motive only hinted at previously is certainly an unusual approach, especially so late in the work. This segment gathers energy toward a climax where the tempo slows to *Largamente* and the Willan motto, in a somewhat augmented form, is powerfully enunciated. Another surprise follows. The horn call (2P) is presented in *stretto* by trumpets, horns, and trombones, a dramatic and unexpected gesture that helps bind the various facets of the Coda together.

Willan has other surprises as well. Following this impressive brass *stretto*, a brief reference to the *Lento mistico* motive brings the music to the work's ultimate climax. In another full-orchestra *Largamente*, trumpets, horns, and English horn declaim theme one from the Adagio, which, of course, was first played as a horn solo. The effect is musically convincing. Additional fragments from the second movement, material from the very beginning of this third movement, including 1M in the bass voices, and another brief brass chorale prepare for a muscular tonic cadence in simplified rhythm.

Symphony No. 1 is a landmark composition in Canadian music—the first full-length symphony written and performed in Canada. Its importance was recognized in the years following its completion, when public interest resulted in the second Toronto performance on July 1, 1937 (Clarke 1983, 32–33). However, as observed during the previous analysis, despite much compelling and energetic music, this work displays a number of structural weaknesses, perhaps not surprising considering that it was Willan's first large-scale instrumental composition and his first significant orchestral work of any kind in more than twenty years. The composer's incorporation of material from diverse sources,

Example 5.26: Symphony No. 1, third movement, bars 345–50 (brass parts only)

which have no inherent, organic connections, gives the piece a rather disjointed quality (especially in the third movement), which Willan addressed, reasonably successfully, through cyclic form. The composer himself provided perhaps the best evaluation. In a 1961 letter to F.R.C. Clarke he acknowledged that his symphony was "an uneven work" (Clarke 1983, 91). In spite of its apparent imperfections, the work's historical importance and its many musical strengths have provided for it a significant place in the Canadian musical repertoire.

Symphony No. 2 in C Minor, HWC 74

Willan's Symphony No. 2 is, as will be seen, a considerably more polished work than its predecessor. It, too, had a long gestation—more than a dozen years. The composer began working on it in May 1936 (four months before completing Symphony No. 1) and had the short score completed by August 1941, but then it was set aside and not finished in full score until 1948 (Clarke 1983, 95). During the hiatus, Willan wrote his piano concerto and the opera *Transit through Fire*.

The first performance, May 18, 1950, was given by the Royal Conservatory Symphony Orchestra conducted by Ettore Mazzoleni, who apparently had assisted Willan with the orchestration. It received an enthusiastic public response, with one critic observing that the symphony "got such an ovation that Dr Willan had to make his way from the balcony to the stage to take repeated bows," although another sarcastically observed, "There was a *fugue* in it, of course." A second performance took place six days later; Geoffrey Waddington conducted the CBC Toronto Orchestra. Sir Ernest MacMillan gave two performances with the Toronto Symphony Orchestra, November 7 and 8, of the same year.[11] In the next twenty years, it was programmed by a number of prominent conductors of Canadian ensembles (Clarke 1983, 43–44, 95, 273), including Geoffrey Waddington, Sir Ernest MacMillan, Walter Susskind,[12] and Karel Ančerl.[13] It has been recorded several times, most recently on CD by the Edmonton Symphony Orchestra, conducted by Uri Mayer.[14]

The first movement consists of a *Lento* introduction and an *Allegro energico* in sonata-allegro form. Although there are a number of thematic elements, Willan's music is thoroughly integrated, so that the movement develops organically from the opening slow introduction through to the final bar. The first two bars are canonic between low and high strings, similar to the opening of the unfinished *Largo for Organ and Orchestra* of 1933.

In this first part of the Introduction, the strings present a "mystical chorus" comparable to those that Willan employed so successfully in his choral music. The composer generates this effect with the harmony, which is created through the chromatic movement of voices, rather than attending to any particular key, and includes seventh chords, augmented sixths, added-note chords, and augmented triads, very few of

Example 5.27: Symphony No. 2, first movement, bars 1–3

which function tonally.[15] The seven-bar theme imparted in these bars (I1) will have structural significance throughout the work, much as did the introductory theme in the initial movement of Symphony No. 1.

Example 5.28: Symphony No. 2, first movement, bars 2–8 (I1)

Willan repeats his theme twice. The first restatement is transposed up a perfect fifth and harmonized virtually identically; the second returns to the original pitches with the melody in the bass voices and is shortened to six bars; the texture is considerably more animated. The music then gathers momentum toward a full-orchestra climax at bar 29 on a dominant ninth chord in C minor, with the first bar of the work in the bass voices. In the following two bars, Willan demonstrates how much he had learned about orchestral scoring in the years since his first symphony. Clarinets, bassoons, and one horn quietly echo the powerful climax—a "splash" of wind instrument sound that provides a pleasing contrast to the string timbre that has dominated the soundscape thus far. Many other examples of similar timbral contrast will occur through the work, adding agreeable variety to the overall orchestral colour.[16]

The end of the Introduction recalls that of the first movement of Symphony No. 1—brief chorales expressed by woodwinds, followed by low brass. As will be seen, Willan continues and expands a procedure in this work that he employed repeatedly in orchestral compositions. Brass chorales frequently function as structural articulations, but in

Example 5.29: Symphony No. 2, first movement, bars 30–32

Symphony No. 2 the composer broadened this concept to often include the woodwinds as well when defining formal elements, another example of his increased attention to orchestral colour.

Example 5.30: Symphony No. 2, first movement, bars 34–39.
Note: The final chord is an open fifth. Cadential chords throughout this movement, and the symphony in general, are often open fifths.

The primary area of the sonata-allegro form arrives at bar 39. At least four thematic elements are presented and, as seen in other works, Willan engages in considerable development of motives within the primary area. The first theme (P1) is highly energetic and clearly developed out of the minor third from the first bar of the movement (Clarke 1983, 96). The tritone skip in bar 42 will have important developmental implications in this and subsequent movements.

Immediately following P1, the low brasses insert a one-bar harmonic "wedge." Brief though it is, this entry functions as a structural articulation between two thematic elements and introduces the concept of the harmonic/melodic wedge, which will be an important contrapuntal aspect of the primary area. It is also another example of effective scoring.

114 This Awareness of Beauty

Example 5.31: Symphony No. 2, first movement, bars 40–48 (P1)

The second element is an extension of the first three notes of P1, but set against its own inversion (Clarke 1983, 96) as the first extended melodic wedge.

Example 5.32: Symphony No. 2, first movement, bars 50–56 (P2)

Following one statement of P2, P1 is repeated in total, but transposed up a tritone. During this iteration, brief, imitative woodwind figures suddenly appear over low-register melodies and string tremolos. The texture of these figures and their fleeting character are reminiscent of similar passages in the Scherzo of the Symphony No. 5 by Tchaikovsky.[17]

Example 5.33: Symphony No. 2, first movement, bar 60

The brass wedge is repeated and ushers in a short restatement of P2 in shifting metre[18] and a third thematic element (P3) that appears to have no specific connection to previous music, although the minor third from P1 is prominent and its texture features contrary motion similar to P2.

Example 5.34: Symphony No. 2, first movement, bars 71–76 (P3)

At bar 79 all rhythmic activity is reduced to a held chord (an open fifth A/E with G in the bass), and a short horn call connects to the next bar. The effect is surprisingly poignant, and Willan uses this horn motive as an important connecting ingredient several times in this movement.

Example 5.35: Symphony No. 2, first movement, bars 79–80 (horn call)

The following bars are a short development using P3 and the third bar of P1 in motivic elaboration of its rising tritone skip.

Example 5.36: Symphony No. 2, first movement, bars 85–86

Willan, however, has another thematic element to articulate before completing the primary area. This component (P4) arrives at bar 93

Example 5.37: Symphony No. 2, first movement, bars 93–100 (P4)

and, while quite contrasted with other primary themes, is related intervallically to both P1 and P3.

A brief development of motives from P4 and P1 leads to a silent bar (after another open fifth cadence), a change of tempo to *Moderato*, and a short reference to P3, which bring the primary area to a close.

The secondary area arrives at bar 110, in E minor, an unexpected tonality, which has no inherent relationship to the tonic, C minor. It has two thematic components. The first (S1) is virtually a quotation from the Adagio of Symphony No. 1, but may also be derived from the fourth and fifth bar of the theme from the Introduction (I1).

Example 5.38: Symphony No. 2, first movement, bars 111–13 (S1)

The second component appears to be related to the tritone motive from P1 that received considerable development in the primary area, with the tritone expanded to a perfect fifth. Interestingly, while S2 is being introduced by first violins, S1 appears in sequence in the bass voices.

Example 5.39: Symphony No. 2, first movement, bars 116–24

Willan does not engage in development as he had in the primary area. The S1/S2 complex is repeated and extended and then the horn call from bar 79 is recalled to bridge from the Exposition to the Development.[19]

The Development returns to *Allegro* and begins with a *fugato*, the subject of which is based on P4. The entire passage is entrusted to the woodwinds, which are supported only by a few chords in strings and brass, a distinctive all-woodwind timbre that may be unique in Willan's orchestral music.

Example 5.40: Symphony No. 2, first movement, bars 146–52

The horn call connects the *fugato* to the next subsection of the Development where the trumpets play a rhythmically altered version of the first four bars of I1, accompanied by downward-sweeping lines that relate to both primary and secondary material. A *rallentando* makes these bars climactic.

Example 5.41: Symphony No. 2, first movement, bars 156–59 (trumpets)

The full-orchestra texture quickly dissipates to an oboe solo that is related to P3.

Example 5.42: Symphony No. 2, first movement, bars 160–65 (oboe)

Willan develops the final motive of the solo with further brief solos on flute, clarinet, and violin, a warmly transparent texture that prepares for perhaps the biggest surprise of the first movement.

At bar 169, Willan introduces a broad, lyrical "English" melody. While new to the movement, this "Development theme" incorporates motives from the primary and secondary areas in both melody and accompaniment, allowing it to evolve seamlessly out of earlier material.[20] This expansive tune, which "unfolds splendidly in E-flat major" (Clarke 1983, 97), is marked *Espressivo e cantabile,* implying a slower tempo. Twenty-three bars long, it appears to separate into phrases of eleven, four, five, and three bars, but the rich contrapuntal texture blurs the phrase endings, permitting the melodic line to develop continuously throughout its full length.

Example 5.43: Symphony No. 2, first movement, bars 169–91 (Development theme)

Willan states this theme but once. A very brief transition takes the music back to P1 in order to increase the tempo to the original *Allegro*. The composer accomplishes the *accelerando* in a masterful way. The first two measures of P1 are presented and then the minor-third motive is collapsed in onto itself to generate a Willan rush that drives the music forward to an enormous climax that dissolves into the Recapitulation. The climactic bars are over a pedal point, but, interestingly, not the dominant pedal that might be expected, but F-sharp, the leading tone of the dominant (Clarke 1983, 97), which generates an unusual progression to the tonic, C minor, for the beginning of the Recapitulation.

The Recapitulation, beginning at bar 204, is anything but regular. P1 and P2 arrive more or less as expected, but after P2 Willan inserts a four-voice fugue on a subject that initially appears to be new material but is in fact a rhythmically compressed version of the complete theme from the Introduction (I1), in D minor instead of the original C minor.

Example 5.44: Symphony No. 2, first movement, bars 219–25 (subject and counter-subject)

Willan, the master contrapuntalist, provided tonal answers and an effective counter-subject, but a fugue at this point in the movement is a rare occurrence, and probably the source of the unknown reviewer's sarcastic comment at the premiere: "There was a *fugue* in it, of course" (Clarke 1983, 44). In context, however, it does not seem so incongruous, since Willan based it on familiar material and echoed the style of P4. After a complete fugue exposition, the composer adds a short section of free counterpoint, and an episode that slides almost imperceptibly into F-sharp minor.

The fugue gradually simplifies and flows into a simultaneous recall of P4 and S1, followed by a truncated statement of P1 in first and second horns supported only by sustained chords in woodwinds and strings. Willan expands the end of the horn line to encompass all the horns and the trumpets in a compelling passage that propels the music into the climax of the movement—a full-orchestra statement of the Development theme in the unexpected key of B major. The melody is altered during its final phrases to maintain momentum and to progress toward the tonic key. Willan winds down from his climax by recalling S2 and the fugue subject in a gradually receding texture.

The Coda, which begins at bar 300, finally re-establishes the tonic, C minor. Essentially only primary-area material is employed, including P1 in inversion and in diminution. However, only eight bars from the end of the movement, Willan abruptly inserts an *allargando*, during which trumpets and horns in unison proclaim P2 without its complimentary inversion.

Example 5.45: Symphony No. 2, first movement, bars 315–17 (horns and trumpets)

Since the music is driving to the cadence at this point, the unexpected material and the slower tempo create a compelling event. Like the end of Symphony No. 1, the final bars are simplified in all musical aspects. Willan repeats a two-chord motive (C minor and unison C) three times in straightforward quarter notes to slow the momentum; however, the cadential progression that follows is extraordinary. The bass line descends in whole steps and then leaps by a tritone to the final sonority, creating a chord sequence of: incomplete C minor^7, Italian sixth intensified to a French sixth, C/G open fifth.

The augmented sixth chord as a substitute for the dominant is unusual, but not unprecedented. One wonders if Willan might have gotten

Example 5.46: Symphony No. 2, first movement, bars 321–22

this idea from Bruckner, who was especially fond of this harmonic strategy (Simpson 1967, 125), and, as an organist and church musician, Willan would likely have been familiar with Bruckner's substantial oeuvre of sacred choral music. Apart from any outside influence, however, the voice leading in these bars is certainly distinctive.

The Adagio, one of Willan's most admirable creations, is called "love music" by Clarke (Clarke 1983, 97). The short score of this movement was completed in August 1941, when Willan was involved in a love affair with a young woman. Clarke believes that this relationship is reflected in the gentleness and expressive beauty of this music (Clarke 1983, 37, 97–98).

Although the movement adheres to no predetermined structure, it appears to be in four parts: $A-B-B_1-A_1$, but the sections are not balanced in either length or function. The A sections are quite short and expository or recapitulatory, while the B sections are extended to considerable length through motivic development.

Willan began the movement with four solemn chords that recall, but do not duplicate, the woodwind and brass chorales from the end of the Introduction to the first movement. They set the mood, and are apparently intended to function as a transition from the key of the previous movement (C minor) to the new tonality of E major. Section A, which begins at bar 3, presents a long, lyrical melody (theme one) in solo horn.

Example 5.47: Symphony No. 2, second movement, bars 5–22 (theme one)

The accompaniment, initially strings only but with the woodwinds gradually added, is a notable example of Willan's contrapuntal skill. The accompanying lines support and enhance the theme, with individual motives responding and sometimes anticipating the melody. Perhaps the best example of this symbiotic relationship occurs in bar six; second violins play the inversion of the first bar of theme one against its second bar in the solo horn. Hints of familiar motives from the first movement also appear, alluding to cyclic form, which will be a major aspect of the subsequent movements.

Willan immediately repeats theme one in first violins. Some phrases are ornamented and it is extended for a few bars to complete the thematic content of this section. Solo horn contributes an especially complementary countermelody. However, although the thematic material has been presented, the A section has a further component. One flute and the two clarinets proffer another Willan fingerprint, undulating parallel sixth chords (fauxbourdon) supported, in this case, by a single descending scalic line in cellos. These lovely measures function like a

Example 5.48: Symphony No. 2, second movement, bars 42–50

codetta, completing the section but also maintaining momentum into the ensuing part of the structure.

The B section, which arrives at bar 50, is marked *Animato* and begins with another horn solo. Theme two is clearly related to theme one but consists of a single four-bar phrase that is promptly developed canonically. Woodwind timbre is emphasized, and Willan simplified other supporting lines to emphasize the variegated orchestral colours. He also gradually compressed the initial four-bar phrase to two bars, and eventually to a single motive as a means of enhancing impetus.

Example 5.49: Symphony No. 2, second movement, bars 50–60 (theme two and development, solo lines only)

A second canonic development begins at bar 66. Theme two, with a slight alteration of its final motive, is presented by solo flute, and then the altered motive is echoed through woodwinds and strings. This section begins to build toward an apparent climax, with theme two in either its original or altered form present in virtually every bar, and fanfare-like figures in the supporting counterpoint. The drive to a climax, however, abruptly breaks off at bar 84, where the B section appears to start over. Theme two is restated by solo horn and developed antiphonally, passing to solo trumpet and to high strings and flutes. The texture gradually accumulates by recalling motives from earlier in the movement, continuing the fanfare figures and inserting a compressed version of the theme in the bass voices. This time, the music surges to an impressive climax with the Willan motto prominently audible in the high voices.

The texture quickly dissipates after the climax, leading to an imaginative transitional section. First, Willan inserts a short segment based on theme two that employs only the woodwinds (with sustained chords in strings for the first few bars). This segment functions in a fashion similar to the codetta that concluded section A, and, since both feature woodwind timbre, this segment, like its earlier counterpart, signals the beginning of a new section.

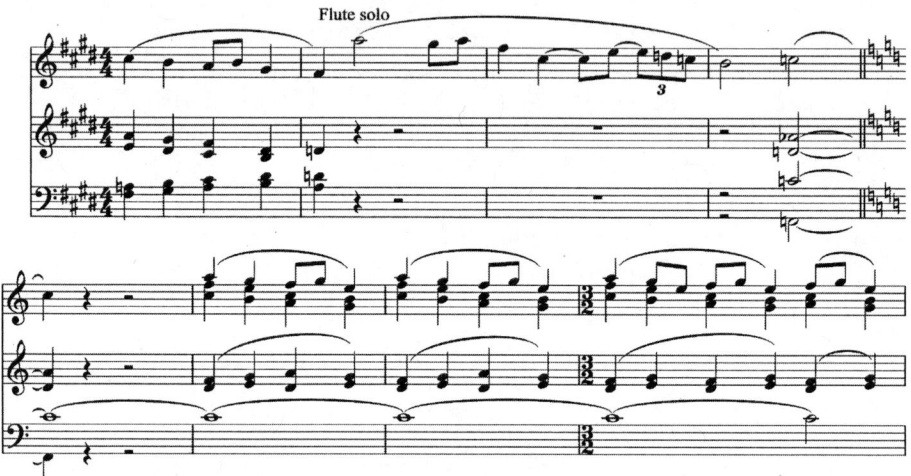

Example 5.50: Symphony No. 2, second movement, bars 101–8

Willan's transition, however, also has other elements. Following the "wind ensemble" passage observed above, he inserts a new horn solo that is derived from theme one and accompanied by a sustained B-flat major-seventh chord in muted strings. A shortened repeat of the wind ensemble passage completes the transition.

Example 5.51: Symphony No. 2, second movement, bars 110–13 (horn)

Section B_1 (bar 116) is shorter than the B section, but is equally developmental in content. It begins with a partial statement of theme one, but Willan does not continue to work with this thematic fragment. Instead, he begins an imitative development of the Willan motto in woodwinds and horns. Underneath the references to the Willan motto, the accompanimental textures of the B section are re-established, and ultimately theme two returns in a rising sequential development that gathers energy to a second imposing climax at bar 138, again highlighting the Willan motto, this time powerfully enunciated by the trumpets.

Like that of the B section, the climax quickly recedes. The Willan motto and derivatives of it comprise the counterpoint, leading to a brass chorale that restates the four solemn chords from the beginning of the movement (Clarke 1983, 98). Since brass chorales so often function as structural articulations in Willan's orchestral music, and because these chords recall the beginning of the movement, one would expect the return of the A section, and, ultimately, that does indeed occur. However, prior to recapping the A section, Willan inserts a transitional segment in which the strings elaborate a pedal C-sharp minor-seventh chord for ten bars, and a solo violin provides a descant that is built from the Willan motto and theme two. A derivative of the Willan motto also appears in solo flute. The effect is magical. One feels as if the music were standing still—a breathless suspension before the gentle energy of the A section is re-established.

When the A_1 section arrives (bar 156), Willan does not recall theme one as it appeared first in solo horn, but repeats its second statement in first violins including the horn countermelody. It appears complete and is extended by the solo violin to another partial iteration. The closing bars present a horn phrase derived from theme one, the introductory chords played by low brass and a rising flourish in solo violin, before settling into a tranquil cadence in E major.

While the Adagio of Symphony No. 2 may well be love music, it reflects not the fiery, impetuous love of youth but the erudite, all-encompassing endearment of maturity (Clarke 1983, 97–98).[21] Musically, it is one of the most effectively integrated of Willan's orchestral movements, but also includes inventive variety in timbre and texture that captivates listeners and performers alike.

The Scherzo of this symphony is unique in Willan's output. He wrote only three other works under this title, and they are short compositions that are not especially light-hearted in character (Clarke 1983, 98).

Hugely energetic, this movement is large-scale, structured in what appears to be a combination of sonata-allegro form and fugue, and full of surprises and humorous gestures. Willan was well aware of the deliberately witty character of the music. He wrote "a! ha!" at the end of the piano score (Clarke 1983, 100), an acknowledgement of its unbridled nature and perhaps an indication of his satisfaction with it.

This movement opens with a one-bar sweep in second violins and a loud *pizzicato* G minor chord. Such short, loud chords, mostly open fifths, in the strings appear often in this movement, functioning as a kind of rhythmic "incision" separating sections and subsections, or signalling important changes in one or more musical elements.[22] In this case, the *pizzicato* chord launches a four-voice fugue exposition that also serves as the primary area of the sonata-allegro form. The subject is an exact restatement of the theme from the Introduction to the first movement (I1) transposed up a perfect fifth, with the metre changed from 3/4 to 3/8 and at a much faster tempo. This masterstroke of musical integration is obviously a component of the symphony's overall cyclic form. Solo flute, completely unaccompanied, presents the first statement of the subject; the answer, in first bassoon and violas, is in inversion. The two subsequent entries repeat the established pattern—bassoon in prime form, clarinet in inversion—and this set of entries constitutes theme one. The only accompaniment consists of pedal tones and a few fleeting string passages, one of which, accompanying the clarinet statement of the subject, constitutes a harmonic/melodic wedge, another reference to the first movement.

Example 5.52: Symphony No. 2, third movement, bars 2–16 (theme one—subject and answer)

These initial entries institute an important compositional principle for this movement. Numerous instances can be identified where the subject and its inversion (or motives from them) respond imitatively or are set against each other in counterpoint.

A substantial episode that follows the fugue exposition is considered by Clarke to be the secondary thematic area. Clarke calls the new theme (theme two) that bridges the transition to the secondary area "the carefree theme" (Clarke 1983, 99).

Example 5.53: Symphony No. 2, third movement, bars 34–42 (theme two)

During the measures that follow, motives from both theme one and theme two are developed. For example, the strings present the first of many instances of fragments of theme one with prime form and inversion occurring simultaneously in counterpoint. In this instance, theme one blends with a motive from theme two.

Example 5.54: Symphony No. 2, third movement, bars 42–46

A surprise is prepared starting at bar 57. A *pizzicato* open fifth "incision" draws attention away from a rendition of theme one in clarinets and sets up a striking unison string passage that is the retrograde of the last four bars of the first statement of the inversion of the subject in the bassoon and violas at bars 13–16.

These gestures prepare the entrance of theme three—a five-bar, dance-like melody in sprung rhythm that arrives first in horns, and then moves quickly through high woodwinds, trumpets/horns, and ultimately full orchestra.

Example 5.55: Symphony No. 2, third movement, bars 59–62 (strings)

Example 5.56: Symphony No. 2, third movement, bars 63–67 (horns—theme three)

It appears that this music is driving forward toward a major climax, but another surprise intervenes. Before the climax can arrive, Willan abruptly cuts off the music in a grand pause at bar 82. The music resumes with another open fifth incision that launches a three-voice *fugato* on the first four bars of theme one in bassoons and low clarinet. The effect is deliberately comical.[23] This set of entries elides into two statements of theme three supported by a swiftly moving canon in violins and followed by an unexpected new theme, which might be considered the closing theme of the sonata-allegro Exposition.

Example 5.57: Symphony No. 2, third movement, bars 104–7 (oboe—theme four)

Willan immediately begins an imitative development of theme four but suddenly abandons his new theme and inserts a repeat that signals the end of the Exposition (Clarke 1983, 99). Interestingly, he does not repeat the entire Exposition but instead returns to what was identified as theme two and the beginning of the secondary area. Presumably, Willan either was concerned about overusing his first theme, or felt that returning to solo flute would undermine the momentum of the movement. Also, to this point in the movement theme two has been stated in its entirety only once. Since it would have an important role later in the movement, perhaps he felt that it needed to be heard again in a prominent place in the form.

The Development commences at bar 120. Throughout this rather extended section, themes and thematic fragments are tossed around the orchestra in a delightfully unpredictable manner. At the beginning of the Development, Willan takes up theme four (closing theme) as if there had been no interruption by the repeat,[24] and then moves quickly through a series of brief subsections using theme one (mostly in pairs of woodwinds with minimal accompaniment), and theme three.

At bar 168, there occurs a kind of "in joke." Willan uses solo oboe to introduce another new melodic fragment that Clarke calls "a parody of the Willan motto" (Clarke 1983, 99).

Example 5.58: Symphony No. 2, third movement, bars 168–71 (oboe)

Willan states it twice surrounded by references to theme one, then jumps to theme two, the first time this theme has been heard since early in the Exposition.

An arresting new subsection arrives at bar 188. Woodwinds and *pizzicato* strings antiphonally exchange phrases that simultaneously present theme one in prime and inverted forms.

Example 5.59: Symphony No. 2, third movement, bars 188–91

The woodwind grouping changes at each phrase: flutes/clarinets, oboes/clarinets, oboes/bassoons, flutes/clarinets, creating an aurally attractive series of interactions. Willan also builds momentum by compressing the phrases from four to two bars. A segment in which theme three is mixed with motives from theme two leads to a full-orchestra open fifth incision on beat one of bar 233. The incision and the ensuing two beats of silence prepare another three-voice *fugato* on theme one, this time in high woodwinds without the comical implications of earlier.

Bar 250 offers another surprise. A theme emerges that appears to be new, although it is intervallically related to other material in the movement. Willan apparently considered it important, because it is developed imitatively for sixteen bars.

Example 5.60: Symphony No. 2, third movement, bars 250–57

Precisely where the Recapitulation might begin is a matter of conjecture. Clarke suggests bar 270, where theme two returns in its most extensive presentation in the movement (Clarke 1983, 100), and the subsequent music does look like the secondary area of the Exposition, but considerably truncated. As it had when it first appeared, theme three is presented four times in accumulating texture, but this time arrives at a huge climax at bar 302. The climax collapses into a brief Coda that offers additional interesting textural concepts. Immediately after the climax, a short descending line passes through a series of woodwind soloists generating a *klangfarbenmelodie* that is again reminiscent of Tchaikovsky, but is also often encountered in the music of other twentieth-century composers such as Stravinsky and Gunther Schuller.

Example 5.61: Symphony No. 2, third movement, bars 302–8

Similar passages appear at bars 316–20 in the strings and 319–23 in woodwinds. The movement ends abruptly with a climactic statement of theme three in woodwinds and brass. Clarke comments: "The listener is left still travelling after the music has stopped" (Clarke 1983, 100), a particularly apt description of this ending. Willan appreciated the suddenness of his conclusion and asked that the fourth movement be started immediately.

In this movement, his only large-scale symphonic Scherzo, Willan ventured well beyond his English roots. With its exuberant, highly rhythmic character, this music seems more North American than English.

The fourth movement, the Finale of the symphony, is the most English sounding of this work. As will be seen, the thematic material and some of the harmonizations are clearly reminiscent of the early-twentieth-century English composers that Willan so admired.

At first glance the Finale appears to be similar in structure to the first movement, a *Lento* introduction and a fast (*Allegro energico*) sonata-allegro. However, closer examination reveals substantial differences between the movements; in fact, Willan's approach to sonata-allegro form is highly individual, more akin to the final movement of Symphony No. 1. Like its predecessor, the components of the form are not always clearly delineated, and, not surprisingly, it also carries the responsibility of securing the symphony's cyclic form by recalling material from earlier movements.

Like other orchestral slow introductions by Willan, this Introduction is largely comprised of slow-moving, non-functional chords that establish a serious, but ethereal, mood. A tonic pedal persists throughout the entire section, adding to the unsettled character as chords clash and resolve against it. The composer introduces two elements that will have further importance. The first is a chorale in the strings that draws the melodic wisps that have preceded it together into a thematic statement (1I). The closed position voicings, parallel movement within the lines, and chord progressions by thirds generate a warm, blended overall sound that evokes passages in Vaughan Williams. It appears twice, in slightly altered harmonizations.

The two statements of the chorale are separated by a quiet fanfare in trombones, tuba, and timpani. These bars employ Willan's favourite fanfare style—parallel root-position chords—but their "distant" quality is unusual and deeply expressive.

Example 5.62: Symphony No. 2, fourth movement, bars 10–16 (1I)

Example 5.63: Symphony No. 2, fourth movement, bars 15–17

Willan repeats and extends this fanfare a few measures later, another example of brass timbre signalling the end of a section of the form, in this case, the Introduction. He also links the two thematic elements of the Introduction by restating the final three chords of the string chorale at the end of the fanfare.

The sonata-allegro begins at bar 28. The primary area has two themes and, like other movements of this type by Willan, involves considerable development. The first theme (1P) is a broad, driving melody that recalls Elgar.

Example 5.64: Symphony No. 2, fourth movement, bars 28–38 (1P)

Willan immediately repeats it, transposed up a tritone, as he had with his initial primary theme in the first movement, and then begins a substantial development of the sixteenth-note motive from the end of bar 31. While this development is proceeding in the strings, 2P, a rather serious-sounding fanfare, appears in the horns and migrates through the brass section.

Example 5.65: Symphony No. 2, fourth movement, bars 49–53 (2P—horns)

Willan develops 2P canonically for 39 bars, while also recalling motives from the first movement, P2 and P3 in particular, in brief connecting passages. The primary area comes to a halt at bar 83 with a quick *rallentando* that indicates the transition to the secondary area. Willan's skill in writing bridging music is amply demonstrated in these bars. A slower and less resolute statement of 2P is followed by a motive in low strings that is derived from 2P.

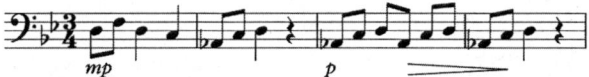

Example 5.66: Symphony No. 2, fourth movement, bars 89–92

The passage that follows is scored for clarinets and bassoons and anticipates the secondary theme. Willan's transition looks both backward and forward, creating a smooth connection to the upcoming secondary area.

Example 5.67: Symphony No. 2, fourth movement, bars 93–97

The secondary area presents but a single theme (1S) at a slower tempo (*Moderato*) and in E-flat major, the relative major of the tonic (C minor)—the expected secondary key in traditional sonata-allegro form. A broadly extended theme, 1S has the character of an English ceremonial melody, resembling those of Elgar and Holst. Willan's melody, however, does not fall into any kind of regular phrasing. It is, in fact, very difficult to determine where the theme ends and development begins.

Example 5.68: Symphony No. 2, fourth movement, bars 101–12 (1S)

Unlike his practice in previous movements, Willan develops 1S for more than fifty bars with no clear cadences. Ultimately, the secondary area rises to a powerful climax at bars 152–53 with the Willan motto in the high voices.

Precisely where the Development begins is unclear. Clarke selected bar 156 and suggests that it consists of only twenty bars, two statements of 1P (Clarke 1983, 101). However, bars 154–55 consist of three short, rhythmically isolated B minor chords that stand out of the mostly contrapuntal texture and would seem to indicate an important structural event. The Development should certainly begin with these bars, if, indeed, there is a Development section at all. The return of 1P essentially complete at bar 156 gives the sense of Recapitulation even if it is not in the tonic key. Since Willan incorporated so much development of both primary and secondary materials into the Exposition, perhaps he felt there was no need for a separate Development section, and the three isolated B minor chords indicate both the completion of the Exposition and the beginning of the Recapitulation.

The tonic returns forcefully at bar 176.[25] The thematic material is the string chorale from the Introduction to this movement, rescored for woodwinds and brass, over an energetic string tremolo tonic pedal. The tempo is reduced to *Largamente* to ensure that the aural connection will be apparent, and these measures comprise the climax toward which the two statements of 1P (or the entire Development) were leading. At bar 190, the brass present, in exactly the same voicing, the four solemn chords from the beginning of the Adagio, although the fourth chord is in major, rather than minor, mode. At the same time, the strings in unison introduce what seems to be a new thematic idea, built from a combination of earlier motives.

Example 5.69: Symphony No. 2, fourth movement, bars 190–93

Recapitulation is truly underway by bar 194 where the transition from the Exposition reappears, leading to a recall of 1S complete, but in E major instead of E-flat or C minor. As it had in the Exposition, the music rises to a grand climax with the Willan motto, which this time is extended for sixteen bars. Clarke considers these sixteen bars to be the climax of the entire symphony (Clarke 1983, 102).

The Coda arrives at bar 272 with another confirmation of cyclic form. In full orchestra, and at a much slower tempo (*Molto largemente*), a major mode (C major) version of the theme from the Introduction to the first movement (I1) returns in climactic fashion. A principal integrating feature of the entire symphony, this theme has appeared in all movements except the Adagio. It segues into fragments of primary material from the first movement; P2 appears in *stretto* in the brass, while the high voices proffer a sequential motive from P1. Bars 288–91 present a triplet passage in parallel sixth chords that recall the closing part of the A section of the second movement. The cadential section is virtually a quotation of the ending of the first movement, including the dramatic trumpet and horn declamation of P2, but transposed to the major mode. Unlike the first movement, however, the final progression is three straightforward C major chords.

Symphony No. 2 is one of Willan's most impressive achievements. He was fully in command of the orchestral medium in terms of form, thematic material, and scoring. This symphony also shows the effects of his three decades in North America. Willan surely was aware of the growing accomplishments of American composers such as Aaron Copland, William Schuman, and Wallingford Riegger during the 1930s and 40s, as well as their interest in shifting metre and the impact of dance rhythms such as those of jazz on their concert music. In Willan's Symphony No. 2 one can see their influence in the unexpected metre changes in the first movement, and in the sprung rhythm in the *Scherzo*.

PART TWO

"A Couple of Very Pretty Tunes": Works for Wind Band

Willan's catalogue of compositions contains three pieces for concert band (two shorter works and one large-scale composition), a group of outstanding brass/percussion fanfares, and a curious work for percussion ensemble that was clearly intended for pedagogical purposes. Most of these compositions date from rather late in Willan's career. With the exception of the percussion ensemble composition, which is an anomaly in the composer's oeuvre and dates from 1938, the earliest works were written in 1949, shortly before his retirement from the University of Toronto, and the latest appeared in 1967, less than a year before his death.

Like most of his orchestral compositions, Willan's wind band music has not achieved the enduring international recognition awarded to his choral compositions. *Royce Hall Suite* did receive reasonably frequent performances in Canada, the United States, and England for a number of years after its publication in 1952, but it has essentially disappeared from concert programs and is currently out of print. *Élégie héroïque* was popular with Canadian band conductors for at least twenty years after its publication in 1971 but is seldom heard today; it, too, has recently gone out of print.[1] The band version of the *Centennial (Ceremonial) March* is nothing short of obscure. To date, it remains in manuscript and has received but two performances. Scores and parts of this march have recently been deposited in the National Library of Canada and in the Canadian Music Centre (Toronto), which hopefully will bring it to the attention of the band community, at least in Canada. None of Willan's fanfares have been published and are available only from the National Library of Canada. Performances of them are rare, despite their exceptional quality. The percussion ensemble work was published shortly after its composition and seems to have enjoyed considerable popularity among music teachers, but has since fallen into obscurity.

6

Concert Band Works

The composer scored none of the concert band works himself. His confidence in his ability to score orchestral compositions apparently did not extend to works for band. For two of them, *Royce Hall Suite* and *Élégie héroïque*, he produced a short score, which was then orchestrated by an editor and a band conductor respectively. As will be seen, this procedure did not serve Willan's music especially well. The third work, *Ceremonial March for the Canadian Centennial*, was originally scored for orchestra and transcribed for band in unusual circumstances. Fortunately, the arranger, Captain Charles Adams, produced a superb transcription that preserved the character of Willan's music and employed the band instrumentation with insight and finesse.

Royce Hall Suite, HWC 78

Royce Hall Suite is Willan's major contribution to the concert band repertoire. During the summers of 1948 and 1949, Willan taught courses in choir and church music at the University of California, Los Angeles (UCLA). While there, he met Patton McNaughton, conductor of the UCLA Concert Band, who asked him to write a band work (Clarke 1983, 42–43). Willan composed his first band piece early in 1949, selecting as his title the name of the concert hall on the UCLA campus. McNaughton and the UCLA Concert Band premiered the three-movement suite in Royce Hall in May 1949;[1] Howard Cable[2] conducted the Canadian premiere on August 3, 1952 (Bryant 1972, 43). Since Willan provided only a short score, McNaughton apparently wrote out a set of parts for the premiere. Presumably, these were sent to the publisher when Associated Music Publishers (AMP), then a subsidiary of BMI, accepted the work for publication in 1952. AMP engaged William Teague, a staff arranger for BMI Publications, to edit and score the suite.[3]

William Teague was well known in the band world. During the 1930s and 40s he had produced numerous arrangements for band, primarily of the popular music of the time by George Gershwin, Victor Herbert, Cole Porter, and Vincent Youmans, among others. These arrangements were very well received, still exist in large band libraries all over North America, and continue to be performed.[4] By 1950, Teague was in charge of the arranging department for BMI, BMI Canada, and AMP in New York. In a letter to Willan, dated November 10, 1950, Teague confirmed his position at BMI and asserted: "I do all the actual arranging (but the Editor usually has to mess up my work just to assert himself) and try to carry out the composer's intentions." He included his score of the third movement, Rondo, with this letter, and indicated that the three movements of the suite were done separately: "sandwiched in between editing and preparing many other things."[5] Despite his experience and facility in band arranging, Willan's highly contrapuntal music provided Teague with considerable challenges, which he was not entirely successful in resolving.[6]

There appears to have been considerable communication between Willan and Teague during the process of preparing the score. The letter referred to above provides a number of interesting details:

> Please don't hesitate to correct me if your composition is distorted, because I am in doubt about a few places such as the melodic line of the Cornet I, Trumpet I, and Baritone. [*Teague is referring here to the third movement, "Rondo." Unfortunately, he does not specify any particular places where he was concerned.*] Many thanks for your expressions of confidence in my ability and sincerity. I believe I have done my best to honor the name of Willan and trust that the work will be well received by the listening, performing and buying factions.

Teague goes on to discuss the Goldman Band of New York and indicates he hopes to "see that your Suite will be played next summer if the parts are ready in time."[7] Apparently the parts were not ready for the Goldman Band's 1951 summer season,[8] since the published score is dated 1952.

In addition to the letter quoted above, the holograph score in the National Library of Canada has attached a three-page document in Willan's handwriting and on University of Toronto, Faculty of Music, letterhead.[9] This document is apparently a set of suggestions about the scoring of this work, prepared by the composer for Teague's use. Unfortunately, the document is incomplete (only the pages referring to the Menuet and the Rondo are extant), is unsigned and undated, although presumably it was written prior to Willan's retirement from the University of Toronto in June 1950. Teague both followed and deviated from Willan's suggestions. For example, in relation to the Menuet, Willan asked that the scoring be "light and graceful"; Teague scored it for a smaller ensemble that includes woodwinds and horns only. Willan suggested that "flute, oboe and bassoon might be effective up to bar 25," which comprises the opening section of the music. Teague employed flute, English horn, and bassoon, which produces a similar timbre, but perhaps is more difficult to blend. And he altered the scoring dramatically from phrase to phrase during this section, which differs from Willan's suggestion but supports the composer's closing comment on this movement: "The phrasing is very important in this movement." Willan requested that measures 30–41 be scored differently from the beginning; Teague complied by setting the first and last phrases for clarinets only, with the intervening phrase recalling, but not duplicating, the timbre of the beginning.

The Rondo offers a few additional compliances and digressions between composer and arranger. Willan asked that the section beginning at measure 26 be "light";[10] Teague abruptly reduced the orchestration from full band to oboes and horns only. The composer drew attention to a new contrapuntal entity, a rising chromatic scale, at bars 31–32, requesting that this "inner part" be "prominent"; Teague scored this part for first horn to ensure that it would be heard. At measure 78, Willan recommended "very smooth and delicate—'Mozartian' scoring!"; Teague employed a small group of instruments (baritone and cornet solo, four horns and bassoons), which may be "Mozartian," but at the same time he completely changed the composer's registration by transposing everything down by more than an octave. Nothing in the music suggests that this was necessary or desirable. Willan requested that at bar 94 "the theme be prominent in the middle part in contrast to the preceding"; Teague scored this section exactly the same as bar 78. According to Willan, the second beat at bar 147 should be "almost a pause with *sff*"; Teague marked this beat *tenuto*, which is a reasonable choice and is what appears in the original score; however, a fermata with the additional notation "short" might better represent the composer's intention, especially since Teague had already marked the second beat of bar 136 with a *tenuto* that does not originate in Willan's score or his suggestions.

In addition to those concerns discussed above, other aspects of Teague's scoring were promptly identified as problematic. Most obviously, he altered Willan's key structure. The holograph score shows the first and last movements in B-flat major with the Menuet in the relative minor, G minor. For no apparent reason, Teague altered the keys to F major and A minor respectively, which have no inherent relationship to each other. Shortly after the work was published, Willan sent the score to Captain Charles O'Neill[11] requesting comments. O'Neill's handwritten response is preserved with the holograph score in the National Library of Canada,[12] and his observations are generally critical. In fact, O'Neill's concluding comment, "The scoring is about the average—perhaps a little better than the average—turned out by the American Band men," seems self-serving and condescending to his American colleagues. On the other hand, his observations are perceptive and reflect his expertise with the band medium. In relation to the Prelude, O'Neill suggested that the bass line was doubled up the octave rather than the more usual down the octave; however, a comparison of the published score with the holograph seems to show that Teague doubled the bass line at the octave below. O'Neill also mentioned doubling the upper voices an octave lower as a problem. The published score clearly supports this observation. In the first few bars, the soprano line appears in the horns, two octaves below the flutes and one octave below the clarinets and trumpets. Forcing all the parts into the middle register in this way is probably the source of the difficulties with clarity, balance, and resonance that conductors have always experienced with this edition.

O'Neill had some discerning criticisms of the scoring of the Fugue. He noted that "There is not enough use made of the basses." Several places can be identified where Teague transposed low-register pedal tones up the octave, essentially muting their effect. However, it should be noted that in Willan's original score the tessitura of the Fugue is rather consistently high, precluding any extensive use of bass instruments. O'Neill saw balance problems, and the exposition is a good illustration of his concern. Teague scored this five-voice exposition as follows: first voice for flutes and E-flat clarinet; second voice for first clarinets; third voice for second clarinets; fourth voice for third clarinets; fifth voice for alto and bass clarinets. It is immediately apparent that the third and alto/bass clarinet entries will be very difficult to project through the accumulating texture and should be reinforced, presumably by saxophones. However, O'Neill's most astute comment is: "There seems to be a general lack of knowledge of how to handle the individual voice parts." Perhaps the best confirmation of this remark occurs at measures 55–56 of the first movement. At this point, Willan wrote a statement of the three-bar fugue subject into the middle voices. A partial answer in the low voices beginning one bar later created a successful *stretto* effect. Teague scored the first bar of the subject into trumpets and oboes, but distributed the rest of the theme among the woodwinds, making it indistinguishable from the surrounding counterpoint and obliterating any sense of *stretto*.

O'Neill had reservations about the scoring of the Menuet as well: "I doubt the choice of instruments for the opening of the *Menuet*: Flute, E. Horn, Bassoon not good balance nor good blending and mixing. E. Horn does not fit the part." Throughout the performance history of this work, conductors have often found it necessary to double the bassoon part in order to produce acceptable balance, and the flute and English horn do not blend well. O'Neill's comment about the English horn is difficult to understand, since the part falls into a very good register on that instrument. He indicates that Willan's suggested scoring of flute, oboe, and bassoon was "better," but his preferences for rescoring involved thickening the texture, which may not have supported Willan's concept of this music.

O'Neill did not comment extensively on the Rondo. His summarizing comment is that the "scoring lacks balance and definiteness." What he may have meant by "definiteness" is impossible to determine, but balance issues can be identified quickly. For example, at bar 47–48 a flourish of two sixteenth notes followed by an eighth note is scored for oboes and clarinets on the first beat and answered by virtually the full brass section on the second beat, thereby displacing the emphasis to the weak beat of the bar and creating an awkward, syncopated feeling.

Other comments by O'Neill have been rendered irrelevant by the evolution of band performance practice since the 1950s. He often criticizes the scoring for being "thin," and observes that "for outdoor playing—which bands mostly do," the textures should be more substantial. Today, when bands play indoors as frequently as outdoors, transparent textures are seen as a benefit rather than a liability. Also, O'Neill felt that "There seems to be rather too much responsibility allotted to the saxophones: rather too much of their upper register, for best effect." Saxophone playing has progressed immeasurably since the 1950s. The ranges employed by Teague are easily within the capabilities of most contemporary saxophonists, and assigning important material to them raises no concern among current band conductors.

Royce Hall Suite was published by AMP in 1952 and did achieve considerable success. In 1953, it was included on a concert by the Garde Républicaine Band of Paris[13] given in Maple Leaf Gardens, Toronto, on September 21 (Clarke 1983, 51), indicating that the published edition was becoming known internationally. It sold well enough over the next decade that AMP reissued it in 1964. On April 23, 1964, Kurt Stone, editor-in-chief at AMP, wrote to Willan indicating that the suite would be reprinted and requesting suggestions for corrections. Willan sent the letter to Robert Rosevear,[14] the conductor of the University of Toronto Concert Band, who responded to Stone on May 11 with the information that the set of parts in the possession of the University of Toronto were prepublication parts, and that they did not include the titles of the movements and had a few minor errors such as missing rehearsal letters. Stone replied promptly to Rosevear assuring him that the published parts did include movement titles and that the other minor inaccuracies had also been corrected.[15]

Concert Band Works   145

The titles of the movements show the composer's strong roots in music of earlier times and his aspiration to "add to the beauty of the past." The first movement, Prelude and Fugue,[16] evokes similar works by Handel that Willan, as an organ performer, knew well. The movement as a whole is structured as a French overture, another Handel favourite (Clarke 1983, 111). In keeping with this structure, it commences with a majestic Prelude featuring dotted rhythms in four-voice counterpoint that leads directly to a fully worked out five-voice Fugue at a considerably faster tempo.

Example 6.1: *Royce Hall Suite*—Prelude and Fugue, bars 1–3.
Note: All musical examples throughout the discussion of *Royce Hall Suite* reference the holograph score, not Teague's published edition.

The Prelude is brief—only twelve bars—but the very slow tempo ($\eighthnote$ = 80 in the holograph score) and its grand character give the impression of greater length. Although its intense counterpoint does not permit easily perceptible divisions, Willan repeats the opening soprano motive, transposed up a fourth at bar six, effectively creating a second section. This section is climactic, marked *ff* in the score, and apparently intended to indicate that the remainder of the Prelude is to be sustained at this volume. However, at bar 10 the texture is abruptly simplified to unison rhythm, creating a striking aural event, and a musical moment during which it would be difficult to sustain the intensity of the previous bars.

Example 6.2: *Royce Hall Suite*—Prelude and Fugue, bar 10

In the final two measures the complexity of the counterpoint is restored and Willan adds the directive *Largamente*, evidently to ensure that the Prelude ends with the same intensity with which it began. The final chord is a dominant seventh in the tonic (B-flat major) indicating that the Fugue is to follow without pause. Willan reinforced this concept by adding "segue fugue" to the score.

The Fugue is conceived on a large scale. The subject is three bars long and has a counter-subject that is applied every time the subject appears. Melodically, both thematic ideas are similar to motives introduced in the Prelude, but the addition of syncopated figures makes them distinctive and memorable.

Example 6.3: *Royce Hall Suite*—Prelude and Fugue, bars 16–18 (fugue subject and counter-subject)

As the five-voice exposition evolves, additional lines of counterpoint are superimposed to create a climax at the fifth entry in skilfully designed five-part writing. As would be expected, the four episodes that follow restate the subject/counter-subject construct and/or develop motives from either of the thematic ideas. Willan also includes rhythmic development based on the syncopation prominent in both subject and counter-subject, and often expands the texture to incorporate five independent contrapuntal strands.

A point of particular climactic and contrapuntal interest occurs at bars 55–56, the implied *stretto* discussed earlier, which is further enhanced by an inversion of the head of the subject in the top voice.

Example 6.4: *Royce Hall Suite*—Prelude and Fugue, bars 55–56 (*stretto* effect)

The harmony remains close to the tonic (B-flat major) for most of the Fugue; however, the brief coda, marked *Accelerando* then, a bar later,

Molto rallantando becomes abruptly very chromatic—perhaps more Wagner than Handel—which establishes a context for chromaticisms that will appear in subsequent movements. The uncharacteristic tempo changes may be intended to draw attention to the sudden transformation of the harmonic setting.

Example 6.5: *Royce Hall Suite*—Prelude and Fugue, bars 65–68

The delightful Menuet that follows is in the style of the *Harmoniemusik*[17] of the late eighteenth century. When Teague scored this movement, he quite correctly employed only woodwinds and horns, a timbre that also recalled the *Harmonie* ensemble. Structured in ternary form, this music is almost entirely in three parts, creating a delicate texture that was certainly unusual in the band music of the time. However, unlike earlier music, Willan, as he often did, incorporated unexpected phrase lengths. The A sections are comprised of two thirteen-bar periods, which divide into phrases of four and nine bars. The B section is more regular with periods of sixteen and twenty bars respectively, and phrases that are either four or eight bars, although phrasal elisions give the impression of irregularity. While the two sections are not exactly balanced, they do have similar construction. In each section, the two periods begin with the same music but then proceed differently— a Willan fingerprint. In the A sections, the initial period cadences on the dominant (D major), and the second period returns to the tonic. The B section is in the relative major key (B-flat major) and is slightly more complex. The two periods are elided and the second is extended through melodic development to prepare the return to A. This section also offers a simple but effective hemiola.

Example 6.6: *Royce Hall Suite*—Menuet, bars 30–32

The melody is uncomplicated and gracious as befits its reminiscence of earlier times, but, as is typical of Willan's music at this time in his compositional life, it is derived from the main theme of the previous movement; that is, the fugue subject.

Example 6.7: *Royce Hall Suite*—Menuet, bars 5–7

Harmonically, this movement never strays far from the tonic (G minor) or its relative major (B-flat major); however, Willan's sparing use of the raised sixth and seventh scale degrees in the minor mode somewhat weakens the impression of key and produces a modal quality. Also, occasional chromatic inner lines, anticipated at the end of the Fugue, generate some surprising sonorities:

Example 6.8: *Royce Hall Suite*—Menuet, bars 26–29

This amiable music has its roots firmly planted in the eighteenth century but is never clichéd and sounds completely idiomatic on wind instruments.

The final movement, Rondo, is marked *Alla marcia* and is in the style of a British march. It is, however, anything but conventional. The opening tune, which serves as a *ritornello*, is eleven bars long, and odd phrasings occur often throughout the piece. Not surprisingly, motives from the fugue subject are apparent in this tune.[18]

Example 6.9: *Royce Hall Suite* — Rondo, bars 1–11 (main theme)

The refrain recurs three times. Energetic and forceful, it implies a full band scoring, although Willan's music is mostly in four parts. It consists of two complete statements of the theme that are, however, not identical. The first statement cadences on the dominant; the second begins exactly like the first, but bars 6 to 11 are altered in order to cadence on the tonic (B-flat major). Harmonically, it employs mostly common chords in the primary key, although Willan's fondness for sixth chords is apparent, as well as a few modal progressions.

While the *ritornello* is robust and imposing, the intervening episodes are much gentler, more in *cantilena* than march style. The second is marked *Molto cantabile*, certainly an unexpected indication in the context of a march. Each episode, however, builds to a substantial climax and concludes with rapid scalic figuration.

The initial episode (bars 23–55) establishes the first contrast with the refrain. Quiet dynamics and a transparent texture initiate a reflective mood reminiscent of the Menuet. It has two periods of sixteen and seventeen bars respectively. While much of the first period is over a tonic pedal, chromatic inner lines generate a harmonic context rather more colourful than that of the refrain. During the second period the chromaticism is substantially enhanced so that the climax consists of multiple chromatic lines in contrary motion. The melodic material for this section is drawn directly from the main theme and is developed harmonically in the first period and both harmonically and melodically during the second.

In the holograph score, the second refrain is sketched out mostly in three parts. However, since it is identical to the earlier statement, this would seem to be a type of shorthand on Willan's part, not a suggestion of a different and lighter scoring.

Example 6.10: *Royce Hall Suite*—Rondo, bars 23–32

Episode two (bars 78–109) provides the most substantial contrast in the movement. The music modulates abruptly to E-flat major, the style is defined as *Molto cantabile*, and the melody does not relate precisely to any other thematic material in the work, although motivic similarities provide aural connections to earlier material. A *Poco ritardando* that appears immediately preceding this section implies a slower tempo. Overall, the feeling projected is of the Trio that often occurs at this point in marches.

Example 6.11: *Royce Hall Suite*—Rondo, bars 78–85

This episode consists of two balanced sixteen-bar periods which use the same melody, but, in keeping with Willan's normal practice, the second statement is altered to accommodate a more complex harmonic context.[19]

At measure 110, a twenty-five-bar transitional section is introduced that returns to the original tempo and initially incorporates rapid high-register scalic figuration and intense chromaticism. However, a new idea appears at bars 126–33. These measures comprise a fanfare that employs only three pitches (B-flat, F, C) both melodically and harmonically (with the exception of the first beat of bar 126 and the lower-neighbour E-natural).

Example 6.12: *Royce Hall Suite*—Rondo, bars 126–33

The simplification of harmony and texture creates a dramatic musical event that, when combined with the nimble scalic sweeps that conclude this section, serve as an effective preparation for the final statement of the *ritornello*.

The final refrain is extended by eleven bars to effect a convincing ending. While the textures are simplified, descending chromatic lines generate a series of diminished seventh chords that add substantial momentum toward the final cadence.

Royce Hall Suite appeared at a particularly auspicious time in the development of wind band repertoire. The year 1950 is often identified as a watershed date because around this time many important composers, especially in North America, began to accept the wind band as a medium for serious artistic expression. Paul Hindemith, Gunther Schuller, William Schuman, Vincent Persichetti, Walter Piston, and Peter Mennin, among others, produced works in and around 1950 that are now accepted as cornerstones of the wind band literature.[20] While *Royce Hall Suite* has not achieved the iconic stature of these other works, its neoclassical nature matches well with many of them, and, despite its less-than-acceptable scoring, it stands up satisfactorily in this august company. It is, of course, also a foundational work in the Canadian repertoire for wind band. While not innovative in the usual sense of the term, its seemingly familiar surface disguises a number of subtleties that reward performers and listeners alike. A new scoring based on the holograph score and all available research material is long overdue.

Élégie héroïque, HWC 83

Willan waited more than ten years before writing for band again. In 1960 he composed his *Élégie héroïque* for the centenary of the Queen's Own Rifles Regiment in Toronto. He had a special connection to the Queen's Own Rifles since his son, Bernard, had served with that regiment during the Second World War, and he had dedicated his orchestral march *A Marching Tune* (1941–42) to "All loyal gentlemen, with special thought for the Queen's Own Rifles of Canada." As he had done with *Royce Hall Suite*, the composer provided only a short score, leaving the orchestration to be completed by Captain William Atkins,[21] the conductor of the regimental band. Boosey and Hawkes published Captain Atkins's edition in 1971,[22] and it was in print until recently. The holograph score, preserved in the National Library of Canada, is written on two staff lines and four pages. Unlike many of Willan's manuscripts, it shows evidence of considerable revision with numerous corrections, paste-overs, and crossed-out bars. The published score of Atkins's arrangement does not exactly match the holograph; however, a letter to Willan from Atkins written early in 1966 confirms that the men consulted on the preparation of the arrangement, so the composer must have approved the alterations.[23]

Bryant lists the first "concert" performance as November 21, 1971, by the University of Toronto Band conducted by Robert Rosevear (Bryant 1975, 44); however, the work's actual first performance took place long before that date. Atkins conducted his own scoring at the anniversary celebration on April 26, 1960, in St. Paul's Anglican Church, Bloor Street, Toronto.[24] A letter, dated May 9, 1960, from Atkins to Willan provides a number of interesting details and indicates that the work was immediately well received:

I want to let you know how much it meant to the members of my band to have you compose the work for them and then to have you attend the rehearsal of it. The band room is too small of course to do justice to the sound you intended and our playing of it at St. Paul's was so much better. I do wish you had been there to hear it. Many people have spoken or telephoned me to say how much they enjoyed it. Perhaps I can arrange with Archdeacon Swanson to play it again at St. Paul's when a convenient time for you to be there can be scheduled. Will Croombs of Boosey & Hawkes has telephoned me to say how much he liked the new composition at the church and suggested a tape be made of it with a possibility of you granting permission to him to approach his London office about publishing the work. Would you permit us to do this?

... Thank you so much for the Elegy and the Fanfares[25] ... I have derived a great deal of personal satisfaction in playing them with my band as it is rare indeed for us to have our greater composers write for the band medium.[26]

Despite the enthusiasm for Willan's new band work, it took more than a decade for it to be published. Willan received the following letter from C.I Jones, Lieutenant Colonel and Commanding Officer of the Queen's Own Rifles, written on January 4, 1966:

In 1960 you did us the great honour of composing and presenting to us the Concert March "HEROIQUE" to commemerate [sic] the 100th Anniversary of the Queen's Own Rifles of Canada.

This work was played by the Military Band at the Church Service that was part of the celebrations of the 100th anniversary and Captain Atkins has treasured the score since then.

We have now been requested by Mr. W. Croombs, Manager of Boosey & Hawkes, to permit them to reproduce the march for playing at the Massed Band Concert in 1967 for Canada's Centennial.[27] We believe that this would become a significant contribution to Canadian Art.

Captain Atkins would be pleased to be allowed to re-arrange the music for playing by a much larger band; but we hesitate to proceed without your permission.

Willan gave his permission immediately, as is confirmed by another letter from Lt. Col. Jones dated January 10, 1966. Atkins promptly wrote to the composer indicating that he was looking forward to "preparing the score for publication," and that "Will Croombs wanted the arrangement as soon as possible." He added that he was very busy until Easter (April 10 in 1966) and would not be able to work on it until then. He requested a meeting with Willan on April 13, to "go over the score with you once again."[28] This comment confirms that Atkins had consulted the composer during the initial process of orchestrating the piece, but no extant documentation substantiates that the meeting on April 13 actually occurred.[29] Given the publisher's interest in the work and the energy expended by Atkins on its preparation, it seems surprising that Boosey & Hawkes did not release the published edition until 1971.

Élégie héroïque is essentially a slow march, but the harmonic/rhythmic tension created by multiple lines of counterpoint prevents it from falling into the regular phrasing that might be expected. Constant rhythmic movement in the inner lines provides little sense of cadence. The harmony is grounded on D-flat (the initial key signature is D-flat major), but, as is usual in Willan's music, modal elements, added-note chords, and unresolved sevenths obscure the sense of tonal centre. Since few dominant-functioning chords appear and B-flat minor triads are plentiful, major/minor mode is rendered ambiguous. While the work is sectionalized, melodic lines are built from similar material, creating considerable musical unity. Contrast is provided by a distinctive trumpet fanfare that appears immediately and recurs at virtually every structural articulation, a slightly different application of a principle that occurs regularly in Willan's orchestral music. Ultimately, a striking change of key adds another contrasting element.

The Introduction is eleven bars long. It consists primarily of a bright trumpet fanfare, supported by timpani (like many other Willan instrumental works, it opens with a solo timpani roll), which is comprised almost exclusively of D-flat major and B-flat minor triads in root position (with a few passing E-flat minor triads, also in root position).[30] The relationship between these two chords has long-range harmonic and structural implications since it is often difficult to determine whether the key is D-flat major or B-flat minor, and at almost the exact midpoint the key changes from D-flat major to B-flat major, a tonal association established immediately in the first few bars.

Example 6.13: *Élégie héroïque*, bars 1–7 (fanfare)

The first thematic area ("A") is short (bars 11–20) but establishes the lyricism that characterizes all of the melodic material and institutes the contrapuntal texture that will predominate throughout the work. Motives from this theme appear in both the second theme and in its counterpoint. It concludes at bar 20 in a single low-register line that clearly signals a new event.

Example 6.14: *Élégie héroïque*, bars 11–20 (theme one)

The B section is much longer (bars 20–45). Willan placed his melody in the tenor voice, and Atkins, quite correctly, scored it in euphonium. Because of the paucity of clear cadence points and the constant contrapuntal movement in the accompanying voices, phrasal cadences are difficult to determine; however, the melody falls into two phrases of nine and sixteen bars respectively. At the conclusion of this section Willan simplified the texture and rhythm into a dominant–tonic cadence in D-flat major.

A dramatic transitional section (bars 45–65) next appears. It begins by repeating the fanfare from the opening bars, then extending it

Example 6.15: *Élégie héroïque*, bars 20–45 (theme two)

through melodic development to eleven bars. It is clearly not coincidental that this matches the length of the Introduction since the melody and the principal countermelody of the next subsection (bars 56–64) are derived from theme one.

Example 6.16: *Élégie héroïque*, bars 56–64 (melody and countermelody)

While the fanfare establishes D-flat major, the extension quickly introduces modal progressions that blur the tonal centre and prepare for the next subsection. At bar 56, the key signature abruptly becomes that of B-flat major, but, even though the remaining bars of this section are over an F pedal, the harmony is complex and does not adhere to the apparent key. Atkins marked this subsection *Animato* and *Cresc poco a poco*, neither of which appear in Willan's original, but do seem well suited to the music.

The ultimate climax arrives at bar 65. The key signature indicates B-flat major, and much of the harmony functions within that key, although constant movement in the inner voices and modal progressions link this music to earlier material. The main melody is theme two presented in its entirety in the major mode and with a largely new contrapuntal texture. Atkins marked this section *Grandioso*, another notation not in Willan's holograph, but appropriate to the music's style and supportive of the work's ceremonial purpose. An exuberant coda based on the fanfare brings the composition to a close.

Élégie héroïque was immediately popular, at least with Canadian band conductors. Its dramatic nature, tight musical integration, and warm, resonant melodies make it a highly successful concert work. While the Queen's Own Rifles may have wanted a ceremonial march that they could perform in parades when they commissioned Willan, it is doubtful that music of this contrapuntal complexity and lyricism could be successfully performed on the march, and it has rarely, if ever, been presented in that setting. However, according to Atkins, it apparently did serve its original purpose very well when performed at the Anniversary Ceremony in St. Paul's Church. Atkins's scoring, while generally effective and supportive of the composer's ideas, is unremittingly dense, undoubtedly because the arranger wanted it to be workable in outdoor venues, where it has often been presented. For indoor concert performances the music can benefit from judicious editing.

Ceremonial March for the Canadian Centennial, HWC 84a[31]

As noted earlier in the review of the orchestral version of this march, Willan, as one of Canada's best-known composers, was asked to contribute to the centennial of the country's confederation in 1967. He responded with two works: the *Centennial Anthem*, which was performed on Parliament Hill in Ottawa on the eve of the Centennial, December 31, 1966, and the *Centennial March* or *Ceremonial March*, which was his last work for orchestra but received its first performance in a band transcription (Clarke 1983, 64, 66).

By 1967, Willan was in his eighty-seventh year and struggling with a number of health problems, not the least of which was failing eyesight. Composition of the march took longer than expected, and by the time it was completed it was too late for it to fulfill its original purpose—to be played by professional orchestras in every region of Canada—since the season had concluded for most professional orchestras. However, the Centennial Commission was determined that Willan's march should be performed during the centennial year and turned to the military for assistance, which lead to a rather unusual premiere for the work.

The regimental band of the Canadian Guards, normally stationed at Camp Petawawa, about 100 kilometres northwest of Ottawa, was posted to the capital city for the entire summer of 1967 to perform the enormous amount of ceremonial duty connected with the arrivals and departures of dignitaries as well as numerous special events.[32] The conductor of the Canadian Guards Band, Captain Charles A.W. Adams,[33] was ordered by Army Command to transcribe Willan's march and perform it on Parliament Hill on July 1, Canada's national holiday. Adams received a copy of the score only about a week before the performance date and worked feverishly to prepare the transcription. He concentrated on the band parts and wrote only a rough score for his own use.[34] At the last minute, the authorities realized that the elaborate (and expensive!) programs for the ceremony on Parliament Hill were already printed and there was no place for the march. Adams finally performed it with his band on a concert given in the Centennial Centre, Ottawa, in August 1967.[35] The second performance took place on November 21, 2004, at McMaster University, Hamilton, Ontario. The performers were the McMaster University Concert Band conducted by the author.[36]

Since his march was intended for patriotic purposes, Willan, not surprisingly, turned again to British models, in this case specifically to Edward Elgar's *Pomp and Circumstance March No. 1*. The form and musical content of *Ceremonial March for the Canadian Centennial*, and its relationship to Elgar's march, were analysed earlier in this book and need not be replicated here. However, a restatement of the overall structure is provided to furnish a context for the following remarks: Introduction, first strain (with two themes), Trio, restatement of the first strain, Coda.

In transcribing the Introduction, Adams judiciously retained Willan's opening two-bar timpani solo and closely followed the original scoring during the modified "Willan rush," with the clarinets standing in for first violins. The energetic first theme is in antecedent (4 bars)/consequent (7 bars) form.

Example 6.17: *Ceremonial March for the Canadian Centennial*, bars 13–23 (theme one). Note: The musical examples from the analysis in the orchestral section are duplicated here to facilitate reading and understanding.

In Willan's orchestral original, the antecedent and consequent phrases are scored differently—the antecedent appears in clarinets and bassoons, the consequent in strings. In his band transcription, Adams scored the antecedent for saxophones, a striking and effective timbre, and at the consequent phrase, the clarinets join the saxophones, an alteration that reflects Willan's string scoring at this point and employs the saxophone sound as a unifying timbral thread. Willan scored the repeat of theme one similarly to its first statement but added oboes to the antecedent phrase and the full woodwind section to the consequent. Adams retained the oboes for the antecedent of the repeat but added muted trumpets and trombones to the melody, an instrumental colour that provides a remarkable contrast to previous material. Like Willan's original, the consequent employs the full woodwind section, providing a thicker texture that relates through sound colour to the first phrase and to the previous statement. Theme one recurs for a third time at the end of the first strain, at which point Adams scored the antecedent again for trumpets[37] and trombones, but without the mutes, and the consequent similarly to the two previous statements. In the band version, the three statements of this theme each begin with a different tone colour, but the scoring of the consequent phrases also maintain timbral unity, an insightful use of the colour possibilities inherent in the band instrumentation that simultaneously secures musical integration.

As observed in the earlier analysis of this march, Willan's transition between theme one and theme two of the first strain includes two brief, but arresting, polytonal passages in brass-only scorings.

In his band transcription, Adams carefully preserved the scoring and the voicing of these remarkable harmonic moments, with high-register trumpets enhancing the dissonant "bite" of the polychords.

Example 6.18: *Ceremonial March for the Canadian Centennial*, bars 37–38

The lyrical second theme (marked *Cantabile* in the orchestral score) is more regular in phrasing, comprising a single twelve-bar statement. Adams scored it for clarinets and alto saxophones (violins and violas in the original), apparently equating the single reed instruments to the strings of the orchestra.

Example 6.19: *Ceremonial March for the Canadian Centennial*, bars 47–58 (theme two)

Like Elgar's *Pomp and Circumstance March No. 1*, Willan's march has no second strain. A short "vamp" transition leads directly to the Trio, which introduces a majestic ceremonial melody intended to stir the patriotic hearts of listeners. Willan's melody is twenty bars long and divided into two phrases of nine and eleven bars, but these unusual phrase lengths do not distract from the grand and memorable character of the tune.

The Trio comprises four statements of the complete theme in a gradually accumulating texture that required variety in scoring to maintain interest. Adams carefully drew on Willan's orchestration and his textural

Concert Band Works 161

Example 6.20: *Ceremonial March for the Canadian Centennial*, bars 74–93 (Ceremonial theme)

ideas throughout this section. The first statement of the theme is in the warm middle register with a simple accompaniment. In both scores, the melody is entrusted to the clarinets (also violins in the original), which are in their most resonant register. To avoid overpowering the clarinets, Adams employed only woodwinds and horns with a euphonium/tuba bass line in the accompaniment. At the second appearance of the theme, both versions add oboe to the melody and later expand the tessitura by incorporating flutes. For the final two statements, Willan sustained the extended tessitura, placed the melody in the first trumpet, and filled out the accompaniment by adding the trombones and a new series of fanfares in trumpets two and three. Adams duplicated all of these ideas, but also wrote percussion parts that gradually become more and more decorated as this section progresses. Other than timpani, Willan's percussion parts consist of sparing use of bass drum and cymbals. Adams preserved all of Willan's percussion, but his addition of snare drum and an augmented bass drum part contribute considerably to the forward momentum, timbral variety, and grandeur of this section.

The final two sections of Willan's march essentially duplicate those of *Pomp and Circumstance March No. 1*. The Trio is followed by a repeat of the first strain without the introduction. Although not in the orchestral score, Adams inserted a *Dal segno al coda* to avoid replicating the introduction.[38] The work is completed by a substantial Coda at a slower, more imposing tempo[39] that presents the two culminating statements of the Ceremonial theme, then abruptly returns to the original, faster tempo and motives drawn from first-strain material to drive the music to a vigorous final cadence. As was the case earlier in the piece, Adams's primary addition to the coda is a well-written snare drum part that reinforces important rhythms (especially weak-beat accents) and supports the phrasing.

Although Willan relied on rather old-fashioned models, he also imbued his march with his own musical imperatives in effective and affecting melodies, uneven phrasing, and a harmonic context that outstripped similar English grand marches of earlier times. Most listeners would undoubtedly agree with the composer that his march had "a couple of very pretty tunes" (Clarke 1983, 114).

The transcription of this march is the most successful of Willan's three concert band works.[40] Adams clearly understood Willan's "English" style and preserved it in generally full textures; however, few issues of balance appear, and voicings throughout are idiomatic and resonant. He was also able to deploy the timbral resources available in the modern concert band instrumentation with insightful attention to colour, power, and expressivity.

Willan did not hear the premiere of his march in its band transcription, but there is little doubt that he would have been pleased. Adams's excellent transcription effectively captured Willan's style and created a fine addition to the concert band literature that is especially important to Canadian ensembles but also deserves a place in the international repertoire.

7
Pedagogical Music

Willan was certainly not averse to writing music for the training of young or amateur musicians. His catalogue of choral music includes a substantial number of works intended for inexperienced choirs, mostly written during the 1950s, and he frequently expressed concern about the quality of music available for such ensembles. His instrumental music in all genres, however, requires experienced, if not professional, performers, making the one work addressed in this section an anomaly in his output.

Suite for Rhythm Band, HWC 72

This curious work, so unusual in Willan's oeuvre, does not fit comfortably into this book. However, since it employs percussion instruments in a substantial way and considering the enormous role played by the percussion in wind band composition and performance, it seems appropriate that it be reviewed here.

It is not entirely clear when Willan wrote this *Suite*, but it was published by Frederick Harris Co. in 1938. Because it is atypical in Willan's works, it must have been written on commission, but when and how that might have occurred is apparently unrecorded. The *Suite* is scored for piano four-hands and percussion—triangle, tambourine, cymbals, and drums. The score provides no guidance regarding the drums to be used, but since the part is a single line and displays no rolls or rudimental ornamentation, it probably was conceived for hand drum(s) or similar instrument(s) with no snares. The percussion parts are very easy to perform (almost exclusively quarter and eighth notes); the piano parts are considerably more difficult. Apparently, this was a pedagogical work intended for student percussionists performing alongside their instructors at the piano.

The piece is in three movements: March, Intermezzo, and Jig. While the percussion parts are simple, the construction of the piano parts exhibits considerable subtlety, which offers opportunities for instruction beyond performance. The March consists of three strains with Introduction and Coda. All of the melodic material is developed from the same motivic cell, but, as observed in other works in this study, Willan's melodies are contrasted, especially, in this case, through surface rhythm. The common source, however, also allows him, in the third strain, to combine the melodies of the first two strains in counterpoint, an approach to march form that will be familiar to wind band conductors from the music of Holst and which offers excellent potential for teaching listening during performance and communicating an appreciation for contrapuntal activity.

Example 7.1: *Suite for Rhythm Band*—March, bars 13–20 (first strain)

Example 7.2: *Suite for Rhythm Band*—March, bars 45–52 (second strain)

Example 7.3: *Suite for Rhythm Band*—March, bars 71–79 (third strain)

The Intermezzo is a gracious waltz, in ternary form. Here, however, Willan has again explored his penchant for unusual phrasing. The A sections consist of two fifteen-bar periods that include an eleven- and a thirteen-bar phrase respectively, as well as short connecting motives between the phrases. By contrast, the B section, which acts as a Trio, is more regular, with eight four-bar phrases and a two-bar introduction. The melodies are again closely related and recall motives from the first movement.

Example 7.4: *Suite for Rhythm Band*—Intermezzo, bars 3–13 (A section melody)

Example 7.5: *Suite for Rhythm Band*—Intermezzo, bars 34–49 (B section melody)

This movement is also slightly more developed harmonically than was the March, with a few modal progressions and unresolved seventh chords.

The Jig is a four-voice fugue. Willan has cleverly combined the expected folk dance flavour with a highly formalized musical structure. There are three complete sets of entries of the subject, but in the interests of variety, the second set of entries has the subject in inversion and the third set is in *stretto*. A counter-subject is strictly applied against every entry of the subject. The movement ends with a robust Coda in which material from throughout the fugue reappears, and some figures appear to have more of a folk dance character than what one might expect in a formal fugue. The subject displays intervallic relationships to the themes of previous movements.

Example 7.6: *Suite for Rhythm Band*—Jig, bars 1–4 (subject and counter-subject)

Example 7.7: *Suite for Rhythm Band*—Jig, bars 16–17 (subject inverted)

Throughout this work, Willan employs the percussion in their traditional roles and in creative ways. From a traditional point of view, the percussion contributes rhythmic momentum, supports crescendos and climaxes, reinforces accents, and highlights important rhythmic motives. In more creative terms, Willan employs contrasted cymbal sounds, a number of different combinations of the four instruments, and astute deployment of particular timbres in support of musical material.

In the March, the percussion doubles the second piano in the usual "oom-pa" figures that underlie much march music. A clever touch has triangle rolls supporting trills in the second piano, against the rest of the percussion. In the second strain, Willan asks the cymbal player to use a suspended cymbal and strike it with a stick, providing an interesting colour change. Not surprisingly, everyone plays in loud sections and on accents.

Percussion use in the Intermezzo helps support the form. For example, the drums do not play in the B section, and Willan uses different combinations of the percussion instruments to identify new phrases. Here, too, the option of suspended cymbal played with a stick is utilized. An unfortunate choice in this movement is the overuse of tambourine rolls, which persist throughout the last half of the A sections and all throughout the B section. A variety of differing rhythmic patterns linked to the phrase structure would have provided considerably more interest for both the performer and the listener.

Entries of the fugue subject in the Jig are reinforced by contrasted percussion sounds. For example, at the first set of entries, triangle supports the first entry, tambourine supports the second, and drums support the fourth. Third entries are never reinforced by a percussion instrument, although nothing in the music would indicate why this should be the case. The order of the percussion entrances is altered at the second set of subject entries, and the percussion become much more rhythmically active at the *stretto*. Throughout the final part of the movement, the percussionists reinforce accents and highlight rhythmic figures. The figures so highlighted are not those that might necessarily be expected (eighth-note figures on unaccented beats, for example), and the combination of piano and percussion is especially effective in this part of the composition.

Although it cannot be considered among the composer's significant compositions, the *Suite for Rhythm Band* is more musically interesting than might appear at first glance. It is a fine illustration of Willan's commitment to the musical education of young people and, since it appeared in the 1930s, might be seen as a forerunner to the large body of choral pedagogical material that he would produce during the 1950s.

8

The Fanfares

Willan's only other works for wind instruments are fanfares—one very brief; another comprising a set of three considerably more developed examples of the genre that were written for a very curious ceremony; and one short, but complete, sketch. As noted earlier, the composer had a particular approach to these kinds of short, declamatory works that, while not completely original, was nonetheless distinctive and effective.

Fanfare, HWC 77

In early 1949, Willan, the best-known Canadian church musician, was asked to write a fanfare and fauxbourdons for the enthronement of the Anglican Metropolitan of Ontario. The ceremony took place on May 12, 1949, in St. George's Cathedral, Kingston, Ontario (Bryant 1972 and 1982, 43 and 5). The holograph manuscript in the National Library of Canada consists of a single sheet with the fanfare followed by sketches for seven verses of Psalm 24. The fanfare and the psalm settings are in the same key (G major) and share musical material. As will be seen, Willan himself, and other extant documentation, confirm that they were intended for performance together.

The fanfare, scored for four trumpets, is only five bars long, and might more correctly be designated a "flourish."[1] A note in the score, in Willan's hand, indicates it was to be played twice during the ceremony: "At Entrance of Archbishop" and "Improvise until the Archbp [*sic*] reaches the chancel steps—then fanfare. Gloria follows at once when all are stationary." Obviously, the fanfare had to be dramatic but short to avoid disrupting the progress of the ceremony. It may have been performed twice more on similar occasions. A letter to Helmut Kallmann from George Maybee,[2] dated May 6, 1971, provides the following additional information:

> I am enclosing a manuscript of a setting of Psalm 24 with faux bordens [*sic*] written by Dr. Willan for the enthronement of the late Archbishop of Ontario, the most Reverend John Lyons in 1948.[3] You will notice that it is preceded by a fanfare which announced the entrance to the Cathedral of the Bishop and also, in Dr. Willan's own writing, directions to repeat the fanfare prior to the singing of the Gloria. This has been published as an additional item in a set of Introits, that Dr. Willan was kind enough to write for us, by the Western Music Company. In the Western Music Company publication, there is an allusion that they [presumably, the Introits] were written at my request for St. George's Cathedral Choir, but nothing is said of the setting of Psalm 24 and the occasion for which it was originally written. I might say that this same setting has been used twice since that date for the enthronement of a bishop—on June 11, 1952, for the enthronement of the Right Reverend Kenneth Charles Evans as Bishop of Ontario and again on May 18, 1970, for the enthronement of the Right Reverend J.B. Creegan as Bishop of Ontario.[4]

It is not clear from Maybee's letter whether Willan's fanfare was played at these two additional enthronements, or only the setting of Psalm 24. However, it is singularly appropriate for such occasions and demands little in the way of additional performance requirements, so it seems likely that the organizers of these events would have wanted to include it as an enhancement of these ceremonies.

Despite its concision, Willan divided his fanfare into five phrases. The initial phrase employs only closely scored G major and E minor triads in root position. Phrases two and three are, in effect, part of the same musical unit, although in performance the trumpeters would undoubtedly separate them by taking a breath. The chords are G major and C major; however, the C major chords are invariably placed on metrically weak parts of the rhythm and several are in first inversion. Rather than establishing a contrasting key, these phrases create a plagal effect around the tonic (G major). The final two phrases are also musically a single unit and return to the figuration and harmony of the beginning.

Example 8.1: "Flourish," bars 1–5

This exceedingly brief fanfare is, not surprisingly, virtually unknown and is essentially "lost" in the composer's archive in the National Library of Canada. It is, however, bright, arresting music, appropriate for occasions when a trumpet flourish is required.

Three Fanfares, HWC 81

This set of fanfares includes three pieces; however, the manuscript in the National Library of Canada is not Willan's holograph score and other anomalies also appear. These irregularities include: all three fanfares have very specific timings; the first fanfare is in F major and scored for three trumpets and two trombones; fanfares two and three are in B-flat major and scored for E-flat trumpet, three B-flat trumpets, three trombones, and timpani. It is apparent that this set was assembled from separate sources sometime after the individual works were written, a fact confirmed by documentary evidence in the National Library of Canada and the Hudson's Bay Company Archives in Winnipeg, Manitoba.

Fanfares two and three of this set were written for a truly odd event that could only have happened in Canada. On May 2, 1670, King Charles II of England signed into law the Charter of the Hudson's Bay Company, granting the "Company of Adventurers" exclusive rights of trade and administration over the sea and lands of Hudson Bay and all lands surrounding the rivers and streams that drain into it (Newman 1985, 84–87). At the time, no one in London had a clear concept of the vastness of the territory covered by this declaration, and they could not have conceived of the impact that the Hudson's Bay Company would have on the history of Canada.

Buried in the Charter is a curious clause:

> YIELDING AND PAYING yearely to us our heirs and Successors for the same two Elkcs and two Black beavers whensoever and as often as Wee our heirs and successors shall happen to enter into the said Countryes Territoryes and Regions hereby granted. (Newman 1985, 325)

In his book *Company of Adventurers*, Peter C. Newman expresses the opinion that this strange clause reflected King Charles's sense of humour (Newman 1985, 90), and in all likelihood no one in the king's court could have imagined a situation in which any member of the royal family would ever set foot in this wild and remote part of the world. Undoubtedly, the sovereign and those around him promptly forgot about this stipulation in the Charter. However, the Hudson's Bay Company did not forget. For several centuries, it attended to the responsibilities spelled out under its charter with diligence and substantial attention to detail. Speaking in 1981, Sir Eric Faulkner, former deputy governor of the Hudson's Bay Company, remarked that the company kept "stuffed elk heads and beaver pelts" in most of its western stores in case the sovereign (or another member of the royal family) should arrive in any of the territories identified in the charter "because the continuation of our Charter depended on making the presentation" (Newman 1985, 90).

Twentieth-century developments in communication and transportation made it possible for the royal family to travel to every corner of the far-flung British Commonwealth, and visits to all parts of Canada became possible and expected. Between 1927 and 1970, the Hudson's Bay Company presented tribute, or "paid the rent," to a member of English royalty on four occasions: in 1927 to the Prince of Wales (future King Edward VIII) when he visited his ranch in Alberta; in 1939 to King George VI; in 1959 to Queen Elizabeth II; and, for the last time, to Queen Elizabeth II in 1970[5] (Newman 1985, 90). It is the 1959 event that is of concern to this study, since it was for that ceremony that Willan composed his fanfares.

Queen Elizabeth II and Prince Phillip visited Winnipeg for two days—July 24 and 25—in the summer of 1959. As usual, their schedule was tightly organized and subject to strict protocol. A copy of the schedule for July 24, preserved in the Hudson's Bay Archives, shows that the "rent paying ceremony" occurred on that day in Assiniboine Park, and lasted only twenty-one minutes (12:04 to 12:25 p.m.). The accompanying protocol document, also in the Hudson's Bay Archives, indicates that two fanfares were played: one when the royal party arrived, "at the moment of the handshake between Mr. Keswick (Governor of the Hudson's Bay Company) and the Queen"; and the second at the point where the royal party left the stage on which the ceremony took place. Despite the fact that Willan's score specifies trumpets, trombones, and timpani, all of the reference material mentions one drummer and eight trumpeters. Apparently the brass players used a consort of ceremonial (or fanfare) trumpets with alto and bass trumpets replacing trombones.[6] These instruments, with their long bells and banners, were appropriate for such an occasion and would have made a spectacular sight on what was, by all accounts, a warm and sunny day.

Willan's participation in this event was orchestrated by F.B. Walker, executive assistant at the Hudson's Bay Company, and Ettore Mazzoleni, principal of the School of Music, University of Toronto, and a close friend of the composer.[7] Walker contacted Mazzoleni in April or early May 1959 and apparently requested a "special" fanfare from him. Mazzoleni recommended Willan, and on June 19, he informed Walker:

> I thought I should let you know that Willan has written two first-rate fanfares, and the score together with professionally copied parts has been sent to Edmonton.[8]
>
> Fanfare No. I is very bright, for the arrival, and lasts 27 seconds. This, however, could be taken a little faster, and I have indicated a possible cut, so that it could be reduced to about 20 seconds.
>
> Fanfare No. II is more stately, for the departure, and lasts approximately 60 seconds. However, I have indicated a substantial cut in this one to reduce it—only if necessary—to about 40 seconds.
>
> You will have to walk the red carpet, and let Friberg[9] know as soon as possible, because I am disturbed to hear they have a heavy coast tour meantime and he speaks of having musicians come in for the coronation team. He is even worried about an adequate player for the E-flat Trumpet[10]—so, please put the screws on the right boys. We can't have any <u>sour</u> notes.

Only a few days later, on June 23, Walker was able to reassure Mazzoleni that Friberg was confident that the Edmonton musicians would have no difficulty with the fanfares, and that they would be performed complete, without cuts. Ultimately, Walker advised both Mazzoleni and Willan (on July 27, 1959) that the fanfares had come off beautifully and had stimulated considerable comment.[11]

Meanwhile, between July 17 and 23, Walker and Mazzoleni exchanged another series of interesting letters concerning Willan's compensation for these two brief works. Walker asked for advice on appropriate payment. Mazzoleni responded on July 23, the day before the ceremony:

> About Willan I can only say that when I asked him what he would expect by way of an honorarium he was embarrassed, only too happy to have a part in such a ceremony, did not want a fee, but—on second thoughts—his choir funds were very low and they would appreciate anything from five to five hundred dollars! As you possibly know, he has for many years been organist in a small church in one of the poorest parishes in the city, and has had a remarkable choir of largely untrained voices who do a unique musical service on a voluntary basis.
>
> I would say that an honorarium to Willan of $100 would be more than acceptable ... If the H.B.C. were in a very generous mood and wanted to do something about the choir as well, this would be much appreciated but by no means necessary.

In his letter to Willan, dated July 27, 1959, Walker included a cheque for $300. Willan wrote an eloquent letter of thanks on July 31. Indeed, a sum of $300 for one and one-half minutes of music was generous compensation, and Willan, an avid monarchist, was undoubtedly pleased to have participated in such an observance.

These pieces employ Willan's favourite fanfare style as observed in other works in this study—parallel triads in root position and voiced in closed position, often progressing by thirds. However, unlike other works reviewed, these fanfares are stand-alone works and are considerably more developed harmonically and melodically. The first of the two written for Winnipeg, the one identified as "for the arrival" by Mazzoleni and the second in the present set, emphasizes a major seventh chord on the tonic (B-flat–D–F–A), as well as major chords with added sixth, minor seventh chords, and a prominent intermediary phrase in the key of the raised mediant (D major). Interestingly, the dominant chord (F major) never appears. While the harmony is largely third-related, the modulation to D major is via a tritone progression, a Willan favourite, and a delightful surprise in the context of a fanfare.[12]

Example 8.2: *Ceremonial Fanfare No. 2*, bars 8–9

The second Winnipeg fanfare, identified as "for the departure" and third in the current set, is extended to more than twice the length of its companion piece through prolongation by arpeggiation of both the dominant and tonic chords, repetition of motives, and the exact restatement of one distinctive four-bar section.

Example 8.3: *Ceremonial Fanfare No. 3*, bars 16–20

Harmonically, it relates to its partnering work through the use of major chords with added sixth and minor seventh chords, but progressions also include stepwise and fourth relationships. The major chord on the flattened seventh degree (A-flat major), another Willan fingerprint, also appears.

Throughout these two fanfares the E-flat trumpet is used soloistically, presenting descant-like figures. Curiously, the timpani are always on the single pitch D, whether or not that pitch fits the chord. This suggests that only a single timpano was available, although it is no longer clear why that would have been the case. In present-day performances, it would be advisable to rewrite the timpani part to conform to the harmony. However, as noted earlier, the currently available scores for these fanfares are not Willan's autographs. Presumably, the individual who created these scores[13] was working from a short score that included Willan's "standard" indication for percussion—"Drums." Willan may not have intended timpani at all, and, indeed, the performers at the ceremony in Winnipeg would probably have marched into, and out of, place, rendering timpani impractical. For the original performance, a snare or field drum would have been a more logical choice, and thus Willan's single-line percussion part makes sense. However, according to the one published report of the event (in the *Winnipeg Free Press*), "eight trumpeters and a timpanist" were the musicians employed on this occasion.

Although intended for a very specific event, these are highly effective and very well-written fanfares. They have never been published, but are unquestionably worthy of revival.

The first fanfare of the set presents something of a mystery. Its instrumentation (three trumpets, two trombones) and key (F major) clearly indicate that it does not belong with the other two, but there appears to be no extant documentary evidence indicating when it was composed or for what occasion.[14] It is quite short, only eight bars long, and is harmonically straightforward, using essentially only common chords in the tonic (F major). Like other fanfares by Willan, it does contrast the tonic and submediant chords and places the major chord on the flattened leading tone in a prominent position. Another notable feature is a quarter-note triplet, a kind of written-in *ritardando*, in the last bar.

The file containing the three fanfares in the National Library of Canada[15] contains another fanfare sketched out in Willan's hand. Short

Example 8.4: *Fanfare No. 1*, bars 7–8

(sixteen bars), but complete, it has apparent connections to the ceremonial fanfares written for Winnipeg: the key is B-flat major, and, while no instrumentation is noted, the four treble clef and three bass clef parts imply four trumpets and three trombones. The title reads "No. 3 (or 1)."

In this work, the tonic and dominant chords are built up gradually from the root with each part expanding the sonority outward to create a complete chord, which is then prolonged through a triplet figure that employs both tonic and mediant or subdominant harmony.

Example 8.5: *No. 3 (or 1)*, bars 1–5

This procedure happens three times; first on a tonic chord in the treble clef parts (presumably trumpets), then on a dominant chord in the bass clef parts (likely trombones), and, finally, a repeat of the tonic in all parts (trumpets and trombones), with a dramatic *Rall. molto* within the triplet figure to signal the ending.

It would appear that this brief work was part of Willan's sketches for the "rent paying" fanfares, but was, for reasons now unknown, rejected.

Nonetheless, it is effective, but perhaps not regal enough to be played with the Queen in attendance.

Willan's ceremonial fanfares did not completely disappear after the "rent paying" ceremony in Winnipeg. A letter from William Atkins of the Queen's Own Rifles to Willan, dated May 9, 1960, indicates that they were performed during the centenary celebrations of the regiment:

> We used the fanfares at the Centenary Dinner and the shorter of the two for the Entrance of the Bishop and the Field Marshall. I found the only Coronation Fanfare Trumpets available were not in good shape. I therefore had my fellows use their conventional instruments and they played very well indeed. (Maybe I am biassed [sic] of course).[16]

In another letter from November 3, 1961, Atkins again referred to these fanfares: "I am sending along the fanfares as requested. I have sketched them out in score so that folks down South can extract from them the instrumentation they need."[17]

Atkins's allusion to "folks down South" was in reference to requests from the canon and the organist of the Episcopal Church of the Good Shepherd in Austin, Texas, for the use of Willan's fanfares at the dedication of their new organ. The Willan archive in the National Library of Canada contains three letters from Stanford E. Lehmberg, the organist and choirmaster at the church in Austin, detailing the request and the eventual use of one of the fanfares.[18]

The first letter, dated October 31, 1961, simply requests the use of the fanfares and asks that the music be sent to Texas "fairly soon" to allow for sufficient rehearsal. It concludes:

> ... we are fortunate in having some really fine brass players on the faculty of the university here, and those with whom I have spoken are eager to play. We can certainly manage the two trumpets and three trombones which you mention in your letter of July 16. If we can borrow the scores until January or February, that would be fine; if not, I can have the music copied (if that is all right with you) and return the originals to you (or to the Queen's Own Regiment [sic]) immediately.

None of these fanfares is scored for two trumpets and three trombones. However, by this point Willan had not seen the music in more than two years and may have been mistaken in his memory. Apparently, Willan had mentioned in his July 16 letter that the scores were in the possession of the Queen's Own Rifles Band. After receiving this communication from Lehmberg, he ostensibly asked Atkins to return them, which led to the letter of November 3 quoted above. Since only four days elapsed between Lehmberg's and Atkins's letters, Atkins must have worked quickly at preparing the scores.

Lehmberg's second letter (November 11, 1961) provides additional interesting details.

> I am returning herewith the scores of your fanfares: I have made a copy of them and wanted to send your score back before I forgot it.
>
> Even on piano they sound most impressive—especially the longer third one—and I am certainly looking forward to getting the brasses together so that I can hear them properly. I may also play them on the new organ: it will include a large State Trumpet, rather similar to the one at St. John the Divine in New York only on a smaller scale, and the fanfares are just the thing to show it off. I hope you will not mind this tampering with them.

This letter includes the first mention of *three* fanfares. Since Atkins specifically refers to *two* fanfares in his letter of May 9, 1960, it seems that the mysterious Fanfare No. 1 must have been written especially for the band of the Queen's Own Rifles sometime between May 1960 and autumn 1961, and, because he had it on hand, Atkins included it in his full score in early November 1961.

As it turned out, Willan's fanfares were not performed as written at the dedication of the new organ in Austin, Texas. On Ash Wednesday, 1962 (March 7, 1962), Lehmberg confirmed that he had arranged one of them for organ alone:

> I want you to know how much we enjoyed using your ceremonial fanfare when we dedicated our organ last Sunday [March 4, 1962]. Instead of using brasses, I arranged the longest of the three fanfares for organ, with some

parts played on the big Trompette or State Trumpet in the rear gallery. These were the first notes played publicly by the organ, and many people told me how thrilled they were with the sound. We are most grateful to you for sending us the music and allowing us to use it.

After the spring of 1962, no further mention of these fanfares appeared in the reference literature (other than their listing by Bryant in his catalogue of Willan's works), and they essentially "disappeared" into the Willan archive in the National Library of Canada.[19]

Conclusion

The orchestral and wind band music of Healey Willan comprises a significant contribution to the Canadian musical repertoire. *Overture to an Unwritten Comedy* receives frequent performances by Canadian orchestras, both professional and non-professional. The Piano Concerto in C Minor, Symphony No. 2, *Poem*, and *Centennial (Ceremonial) March* are performed regularly, but not frequently. The technical demands of these fine works generally require professional performers, taking them out of the purview of most non-professional ensembles. The other orchestral and wind band compositions, despite their quality and the composer's reputation, currently appear very rarely on concert programs.

To some degree, this situation is understandable. Works like *Coronation March* and *Royal Salute* were written for specific, patriotic events that are difficult to recreate, and currently hold little interest for many Canadians. However, *A Marching Tune* and Symphony No. 1 have no such association and do not deserve the neglect to which they have been subjected. Likewise, the early work *Epilogue* is worthy of revival; indeed, this piece may well be still awaiting its premiere. As Bryant points out, Willan's orchestral style was established early and did not change much throughout his career (Bryant 1975, 240), although technical command of his materials substantially evolved. A comparison of *Epilogue*, Willan's first extended and fully completed work, with other orchestral works throughout his career confirms Bryant's observation. In this early work, the composer was already using fanfares as thematic elements and developing multiple melodies from the same or very similar material—a procedure he was to follow throughout his orchestral oeuvre. High-quality recordings of all of these works would help to bring them to the attention of conductors across Canada and abroad.[1]

The concert band compositions are currently underperformed because of somewhat different circumstances. *Royce Hall Suite*, in spite of its problematic scoring, developed an international following but has been out of print for a considerable time. What this important work requires is not a reissue of the original publication but a new orchestration that draws directly on Willan's holograph and on the comments about it that the composer offered to William Teague.[2] *Élégie héroïque*, an excellent example of Willan's late style, was established as standard repertoire, at least in Canada, but it, too, is no longer commercially available. Hopefully, the copyright holder, Boosey & Hawkes, will soon bring out the reissue that has been promised for several years. The band version of the *Ceremonial March for the Canadian Centennial* has received exactly *two* performances in its more than forty-year existence. Until recently, performance potential was limited by the absence of a full score, but that deficiency has now been remedied, and its availability through the Canadian Music Centre, Toronto, should bring it to the attention of wind band conductors nationally and internationally. Commercial publication and distribution of this superb transcription are highly desirable.

The fanfares have been overlooked primarily because of the unusual situations for which they were composed, and since all of them can be found only in manuscript in the research collection of the National Library of Canada. Few conductors are aware of their existence. While performance opportunities for fanfares are rather limited, these are remarkably successful short works, which, if commercially published and distributed, would undoubtedly attract a considerable following, especially in Canada.

When one considers Willan's central place in Canadian music, his orchestral and wind band compositions, admittedly a rather small part of his total output, assume a place in the Canadian performance literature of far more significance than their relatively few titles might suggest. However, beyond national boundaries, these works also have a valuable role in an ever-expanding international repertoire.

Appendix:
Works Reviewed with Sources

Included in this appendix are all of Willan's *completed* compositions for orchestra and wind band with information about the availability of scores and parts. This information is included to facilitate the locating of performance materials by conductors or researchers who wish to study or perform these works. References for unfinished works are not included, since such works cannot be performed. However, autograph scores of these compositions are available to researchers from Library and Archives Canada.

Early Orchestral Works

[Allegro Moderato], HWC 65, full score, Library and Archives Canada, Mus 1, 1969-1, XXXII, 1

Through Darkness into Light, HWC 66, short score, Library and Archives Canada, Mus 1, 1969-1, XXXII, 2; full score and parts (orchestrated and revised by Godfrey Ridout), Canadian Music Centre, MI 1100 w689th

Epilogue, HWC 67, full score and parts, Library and Archives Canada, Mus 1, 1969-1, XXXII, 4

Works for Small Orchestra

Overture to *The Alchemist*, HWC 4, full score and parts, Library and Archives Canada, Mus 1, 1969-1, III, 2

Overture to an Unwritten Comedy, HWC 79, full score and parts, rental, Berandol Music Ltd. (Berandol also publishes a purchasable study score)

Shorter Orchestral Works

Coronation March (Marche solennelle), HWC 71, full score and parts, Canadian Music Centre, MI 1100 w698co

A Marching Tune, HWC 73, full score and parts, Canadian Music Centre, M 1100 w689ma

Fugue in G Minor, HWC 105, full score and parts, Canadian Music Centre, M 3134 w689fu

Royal Salute, HWC 80, full score and parts, Canadian Music Centre, M 1100 w689ma

Poem for String Orchestra, HWC 82, full score and parts, Canadian Music Centre, MI 1500 w689po

Centennial (or Ceremonial) March, HWC 84, full score and parts, Canadian Music Centre, MI 1100 w689ce

Works for Piano and Orchestra

Piano Concerto in C Minor, HWC 76, full score and parts, rental, Berandol Music Ltd. (Berandol also publishes a purchasable study score)

The Symphonies

Symphony No. 1 in D Minor, HWC 70, full score and parts, rental, Berandol Music Ltd.

Symphony No. 2 in C Minor, HWC 74, full score and parts, rental, Berandol Music Ltd.

Concert Band Works

Royce Hall Suite, HWC 78, full score and parts, Associated Music Publishers (out of print); Canadian Music Centre, MI 1800 w689ro

Élégie héroïque, HWC 83, full score and parts, Boosey & Hawkes Ltd. (out of print); Canadian Music Centre, MI 1800 w689el

Ceremonial March for the Canadian Centennial, HWC 84a, full score and parts, Canadian Music Centre, MI 1800

Pedagogical Music

Suite for Rhythm Band, HWC 72, full score and parts, Frederick Harris Co. (out of print); Canadian Music Centre, MI 1800 w689su

The Fanfares

Fanfare, HWC 77, full score, Library and Archives Canada, Mus 1, 1969-1, XXXVI, 4

Three Fanfares, HWC 81, Library and Archives Canada, Mus 1, 1969-1, XXX-VII, 7

Notes

Notes to Preface and Acknowledgements

1 As examples of quality wind band works produced by these initiatives, consider: Donald Coakley, *Songs for the Morning Band*; Harry Freedman, *Blanche comme la neige* and *À la Claire fontaine*; Morley Calvert, *Introduction and Scherzo*; and Michael Colgrass, *Old Churches* and several other pieces.

2 It is also true that American composers of lesser stature churn out enormous quantities of eminently mediocre music for the school band and contest market, and this does discourage some researchers and composers from engaging with the wind band. However, the best of the repertoire created for wind bands of all kinds in the United States is generally accepted as distinctive and representative of the central tenets of musical culture in the twentieth and twenty-first centuries, although such acceptance does not always translate into the wind band and its repertoire being acknowledged as appropriate topics for serious musicological inquiry.

Notes to Introduction and Biographical Sketch

1 Now the Royal Conservatory of Music, Toronto (Kallmann, Morey, and Wardrop 1992, 1296).

2 Frederick Robert Charles Clarke (1931–2009) was born in Vancouver and trained at the University of Toronto, which awarded him the Doctor of Music degree in 1954. His composition teacher was Healey Willan. He was organist and choir director in several churches in the Toronto area before moving to Kingston in 1958. He joined the faculty of the Music Department at Queen's University in 1964 and remained there until his retirement in 1991. In addition to his seminal book on Willan, Clarke was also a respected composer of choral, orchestral, and chamber music (Eyk 2010, 29).

3 Information about Thomas C. Brown is very difficult to find. He appears in none of the standard Canadian references, and even Library and Archives Canada has been unable to provide much detail about him, his career, or his life, although he is listed as the contributor of a number of articles in the *Encyclopedia of Music in Canada*, 2nd ed. (1992), including the article on Willan. He was a singer who was part of the small group of individuals responsible for the founding of the Festival Singers of Canada in 1954 and sang bass with that group from its founding until 1967 (Pitman 2008, 92–96, 144–45).

4 Giles Bryant (b. 1934) was trained in England and emigrated to Canada in 1959, settling in Toronto. He was organist/choir director at several churches and a member of the Festival Singers until 1970. In 1968, he succeeded Healey Willan at St. Mary Magdalene Anglican Church. He also worked for the CBC and at the University of Toronto. He went back to England in 1975 but returned to Canada three years later to conduct the Festival Singers until they ceased operation in 1979. He remained active in the Toronto choral music scene, with close associations with the Royal Conservatory of Music and the Kiwanis Music Festival. Bryant has also composed several choral works, which have been recorded. His *Healey Willan Catalogue* (see Bibliography) was published by the National Library of Canada (Drynan 1992, 174–75).

5 Willan's parents, like many others in the United Kingdom, gave their son his mother's surname as one of his given names. His distant family background was Irish, which led to his often-quoted description of himself as "English by birth, Irish by extraction, Canadian by adoption and Scotch by absorption" (Clarke 1983, 83).

6 In the nineteenth century, as a result of the Tractarian Movement, certain Anglican churches had abandoned Anglican chant and replaced it with Gregorian chant and with some of the rituals associated with Roman Catholic practices. These churches were identified as "high Anglican" or "Anglo-Catholic" (Clarke 1983, 4).

7 In fact, Clarke reports that when Willan first heard Anglican chant at the choir school at Eastbourne, he found it funny and was disciplined for his outburst by the master. Willan was to later say that this incident may have contributed to his ultimate dislike of Anglican chant (Clarke 1983, 5).

8 Willan was later to recall that this work was "just like Mendelssohn ... I only went to three sharps in those days!" (Clarke 1983, 6).

9 One wonders if it was this intensive work on counterpoint so early in his career that generated the affinity for unusual phrase lengths so common throughout his compositions. Perhaps the need to extend melodic figures

in order to conform to the harmonic requirements of multiple imitative strands established in his mind a comfortable familiarity with phrases of five, seven, nine, etc. bars.

10 William Stevenson Hoyte (1844–1917) received a D.Mus. degree from the Archbishop of Canterbury in 1904. He was the professor of organ at both the Royal College of Music and the Royal Academy of Music and professor of piano at the Guildhall School. A renowned teacher, he counted Gustav Holst and Leopold Stokowski among his pupils. He was the organist at several churches in London but is most closely associated with All Saints' Margaret Street, where he served from 1868 to 1907. http://hymntime.com/tch/bio/h/o/y/hoyte_ws.htm (accessed August 24, 2010). All Saints' Margaret Street was the leading Anglo-Catholic church in London (Clarke 1983, 9).

11 Evlyn Howard-Jones (1877–1951) was a celebrated English pianist who was one of the leading interpreters of the music of Brahms. A highly respected teacher, he also travelled widely as a concert pianist (Richardson 1951, 198–99).

12 Apparently the organ in this church was in a gallery high above the church floor. According to Willan, the London fog would sometimes invade the church, and from the gallery he could not see the choir on the floor below but only hear their voices through the fog! (Clarke 1983, 11). One wonders if perhaps these experiences contributed to an aspect of his later compositional style that has been dubbed his "mystical" style.

13 As observed earlier, in the late nineteenth century the Church of England had split into two camps. A "Protestant" group continued to employ Anglican chant in its services, while an "Anglo-Catholic" group had restored the use of Gregorian chant (although in English, not Latin), which had not been employed in the English church since the Reformation. The conflict between the two groups was intense, leading to street riots. The Willans were staunch supporters of the Anglo-Catholic faction, and some members of the family were actually physically attacked for their beliefs (Brown and Bryant 1992, 1405).

14 Sir Richard Terry (1865–1938) was among the first English church musicians to promote the revival of Renaissance polyphony, especially the works of English Renaissance composers. Among other positions, he held the appointment of organist and choir director at Westminster Cathedral from 1901 until 1924, and was the music editor of the *Westminster Hymnal* in 1912 and 1916. Knighted in 1922, he composed a large body of choral music, primarily for use in church (Slonimsky 1992, 1868).

15 "English fauxbourdon," or more accurately, "faburden," is a texture in which the melody appears in the tenor voice surrounded by counterpoint

in the other voices. It has been used in English choral music since at least the sixteenth century (Kennedy 1985, 237). The modern interpretation of the term refers to parallel sixth chords—that is, parallel chords in first inversion (Apel 1972, 309).

16 In Toronto, Gladys Willan taught piano and coached singers. She wrote two pedagogical books for Frederick Harris Music and was music director for Dora Mavor Moore's Shakespeare productions in Toronto high schools. Mavor Moore was a former pupil (Kallmann 1992, 1405).

17 Apparently, church organists in England at this time often had independent means, allowing them to accept lower salaries than might have been expected. Willan had no private income and was therefore dependent on salaries that did not match his personal needs (Clarke 1983, 14–15).

18 Willan later claimed that he wrote his resignation on October 10 but waited until the twelfth to submit it to give himself a birthday present (Clarke 1983, 21).

19 Willan had a wry sense of humour. Upon being elected president of the Arts and Letters Club in 1922, he set the club's entire constitution to music, including a version of "Nobody Knows the Trouble I've Seen" to represent members who were behind in their dues (Clarke 1983, 23).

20 This concert was well received. Lawrence Mason, writing in the Toronto *Globe* declared: "Until the advent of Dr. Willan, Canada did not possess a creative genius of Dr. Willan's art standard, and today he stands in the front rank among living composers" (Clarke 1983, 25).

21 A newspaper reviewer declared the trio to be "the most important contribution of its kind to British music during the past decade" (Clarke 1983, 19). There can be little doubt that the performances of these compositions in 1915–16 were landmark occasions in Canadian music—rare performances of chamber works written (at least partly) in Canada.

22 Interestingly, the tensions between the "low Anglican" and "Anglo-Catholic" traditions in the Anglican church were transferred to Canada. In 1922, St. Mary Magdalene was viciously attacked in the local press for maintaining the ritual, ceremony, vestments, and music related to Roman Catholic practices. Needless to say, Willan and his vicar, the Reverend H.G. Hiscocks, were unmoved by the criticism (Clarke 1983, 22).

23 Conductors of chamber orchestras, however, would be well rewarded by performing Willan's Overture for the 1920 production of *The Alchemist*. Scored for flute, clarinet, and strings, it stands well on its own (Clarke 1983, 149). Never published, score and parts are preserved in the Willan archive in the National Library of Canada, Ottawa; Mus 1, 1969-1, III, 2.

24 Edmund Horace Fellowes (1870–1951) was a highly respected English musicologist and editor. Educated at Winchester College and Oxford, he was an ordained minister and choir director, but is primarily remembered for his writings on, and performing editions of, early English music (Slonimsky 1992, 527).
25 Sir Ernest MacMillan (1893–1973) was one of the most influential figures in Canadian music. A child prodigy, he was trained in Toronto and in Edinburgh but by age eight was composing and performing in public. Over his long career in Toronto he engaged with a virtual "who's who" of Canadian music and was associated with most of the primary performing organizations in the city, including the Toronto Symphony and the Toronto Mendelssohn Choir, both of which he conducted for long periods of time and is credited with taking to an international performance standard. He was involved with the establishment of the Canada Council and the Canadian Music Centre and was a regular commentator on the CBC. A tireless campaigner for the improvement of music education, he influenced virtually every aspect of Canadian musical life (Beckwith 1992, 788–91).
26 After the performance Willan was given a standing ovation that one critic described as "the like of which has not been given an artist in Toronto within easy memory" (Clarke 1983, 31).
27 This score is now preserved in the National Library of Canada. Healey Willan Fonds, Mus 1, XXXIII, 1.
28 Douglas William Clarke (1893–1962) was educated in England and came to Canada in 1927, first settling in Winnipeg, then moving to Montreal in 1929 to assume the directorship of the McGill Conservatory. The following year he became dean of the Faculty of Music at McGill, a position he held until his retirement in 1955. He was appointed conductor of the newly formed Montreal Symphony in 1930 and led the orchestra for eleven years. A gifted pianist, organist, and conductor, he was also an inspiring composition teacher, producing a number of distinguished students. After his retirement from McGill he returned to England (McLean 1992, 274).
29 Clarke reports an amusing incident that occurred shortly after this performance. Willan left Montreal immediately after the concert to travel to Regina to perform an organ recital. When he stepped off the train in Regina a newsboy offered him a paper. When Willan refused, the clever boy apparently pointed out that his picture was in the paper. Willan bought it (Clarke 1983, 32).
30 Healey Willan Fonds, 1969-1; XXXIV, 5.

190 Notes to Introduction and Biographical Sketch

31 Ettore Mazzoleni (1905–1968) was born in Switzerland, studied in England, and came to Canada in 1929 to become music master at Upper Canada College, Toronto. He also began an association with the Toronto Conservatory (later the Royal Conservatory of Music) that lasted until 1966. He was heavily involved in the development of opera in Toronto, especially the Royal Conservatory Opera School (University of Toronto division). He conducted orchestras, including the Toronto Symphony, all across Canada, introducing Canadian audiences to much contemporary music (Ridout 1992, 823).

32 Conductor, administrator, and performer Geoffrey Waddington (1904–1966) was born in England and moved with his family to Lethbridge, Alberta, in 1907. He began playing violin at age seven and first conducted publicly before age twelve. In 1921 he received a scholarship to the Toronto Conservatory, where one of his teachers was Healey Willan. From 1922 to 1926 he was a faculty member of the Conservatory and later a member of the Toronto Symphony. In 1922 he began a career in radio, serving as both producer and conductor of music shows, that ultimately turned into a long engagement with the CBC. Playing under him prepared a large number of musicians for professional careers. He conducted the premieres of a large number of Canadian works (Kallmann 1992, 1380).

33 The performances by MacMillan are listed on the flyleaf of Willan's score, which is owned by Berandol Music.

34 The writer John William Coulter (1888–1980) was born in Ireland but spent most of his life in Canada. His best-known Canadian work is the historical trilogy *Riel*, but he also wrote on Irish subjects and completed a biography of Winston Churchill (Lister 1988, 1: 525).

35 Lucio Agostini (1913–1996) was born in Italy but emigrated to Canada with his family and became a naturalized Canadian at age thirteen. Although he worked primarily on film scores, he was also an arranger for radio and TV and a commentator on CBC. In addition, he composed theatre music (although his musical comedies have seldom been performed) and chamber music. In Montreal and Toronto he was highly respected for his orchestrations, his understanding of dramatic principles, his ability to work quickly, and his conducting (Corvin and McNamara 1992, 8–9).

36 The performance was conducted by Ettore Mazzoleni, who became a champion of Willan's music (Clarke, 1983, 39).

37 Before he left England Willan had begun work on three other compositions for piano and orchestra, *Ballade*, Piano Concerto in D Minor, and another piano concerto, but left all of them incomplete (Bryant 1972, 42; Bryant 1982, 6).

38   Agnes Butcher was born in Edmonton in 1915 and trained in Ontario, especially in Toronto and Hamilton. She taught at the Hamilton and Toronto conservatories and made her professional debut at Massey Hall, Toronto, in 1935. From 1938 to 1940 she lived in Hungary, studying with Béla Bartók and serving as his copyist and translator. After her return to North America in 1940, she toured widely, promoting the music of Bartók. After 1949, her tours took her throughout North America and Europe. She retired from active performing in 1984. In 1987, she donated a large collection of music, including the manuscript of Willan's Piano Concerto, to McMaster University (F. Hall 1992, 180).

39   Jean Beaudet (1908–1971) was a distinguished conductor, performer, and broadcaster. Trained in Quebec and Paris, he taught in both Quebec and Montreal, but his primary contributions to Canadian music were as conductor and broadcaster at the CBC. He also served as executive secretary of the Canadian Music Centre (1959–61) and music director of the National Arts Centre, Ottawa (Potvin 1992, 95–96). The manuscript score of Willan's Piano Concerto, in the National Library of Canada, has the following notation, apparently from Beaudet: "One of the great pleasures of my 'short' conductor's life."

40   For example, two works were written to mark centenary celebrations: the anthem *Blessed Art Thou, O Lord* for Trinity College and the motet *Great Is the Lord* for the Anglican Diocese of Toronto. Another work, *Gloria Deo per immense saecula*, was commissioned by the Community Centre of the Village of Forest Hill in Toronto (Clarke 1983, 46–49).

41   An old friend, George Coutts, composed Prelude and Fugue in E Minor for organ, and Drummond Wolff, a colleague at the university, wrote *Festival Fanfare*, also for organ, in Willan's honour (Clarke 1983, 47).

42   John Adaskin (1908–1964) was a conductor, radio producer, administrator, and performer trained in Germany and in Toronto. He played cello in the Toronto Symphony and other orchestras from 1926 to 1938 and was a producer for the CBC from 1934 to 1943. On behalf of the CBC he commissioned Willan's *Transit through Fire* and works from other composers. During the 1950s he continued to produce and conduct for the CBC and briefly taught radio and TV production at Toronto's Ryerson Polytechnical Institute. In 1961 he joined the Canadian Music Centre and worked diligently in the promotion of Canadian music. The John Adaskin Project continues to sponsor new compositions for use in educational environments (Kallman 1992, 6).

43 His anthem *A Prayer of Rejoicing* was written for this event (Clarke 1983, 50).
44 Willan was also commissioned by the CBC. His *Coronation Suite* for chorus and orchestra was broadcast in Canada during the coronation service and subsequently received performances in New York, London, and Toronto (Clarke 1983, 50–52).
45 The eminent English conductor Sir Adrian Boult (1889–1983) trained in England and in Leipzig. In a career that stretched from 1914 virtually until his death, he served as conductor for essentially every major performing organization in London. By the 1950s his reputation was such that he received invitations to guest conduct all over the world. He was especially noted for his insightful and expressive performances of the music of contemporary English composers including Elgar, Vaughan Williams, and Holst (Slonimsky 1992, 224). Boult's recordings of Holst's *The Planets* and Elgar's *Enigma Variations* remain among the most accomplished interpretations of those works.
46 The performers were the Canadian duo pianists Margaret and Harry Heap. They had played the work earlier in a recital at Wigmore Hall, London, which had caught the attention of British pianists. Willan always considered this piece among his best compositions and regretted that it received so few performances (Clarke 1983, 53).
47 Walter Susskind (1913–1980) was born and trained in Prague. He was assistant conductor of Prague's German Opera House from 1934 until it was closed by the Nazi occupation, whereupon he moved to England and became a British citizen. He conducted widely in the UK before succeeding Sir Ernest MacMillan as conductor of the Toronto Symphony in 1956. He also conducted the Toronto Mendelssohn Choir, the Canadian Opera Company, and the CBC Symphony Orchestra with which he programmed many premieres of new Canadian music. He was also concerned with the training of young orchestral musicians and was instrumental in founding the National Youth Orchestra of Great Britain and the National Youth Orchestra of Canada, which he conducted during the inaugural 1960–64 sessions and the 1966 European tour. In 1968, he moved to the United States (Corvin 1992, 1266).
48 He was invited to Ottawa to attend the lighting of the centennial candle on December 31, 1966, but declined. To a friend he confided: "If it were a barrel of gunpowder I might give it serious consideration" (Clarke 1983, 65).
49 Willan claimed that he couldn't play his own major works for organ (Brown and Bryant 1992, 1406).

50 Elmer Iseler (1927–1998) is often described as the pre-eminent Canadian choral conductor of his generation. He received a B.Mus. from the University of Toronto in 1950, and by 1954 was already assistant conductor of the Toronto Mendelssohn Choir. That same year, he helped to found the Festival Singers of Canada and conducted them for twenty-four years. He assumed directorship of the Toronto Mendelssohn Choir in 1964 and held that position until 1997. In 1978, he founded the Elmer Iseler Singers, a professional chamber choir. In addition to conducting, he actively commissioned and recorded new works, and toured and broadcast with his choirs. He received many honours, including the Canada Council Medal and the Order of Canada (M. McLean 1992, 638).

51 Composer Godfrey Ridout (1918–1984) studied with Healey Willan at the Toronto Conservatory and largely adopted Willan's creed of "adding to the beauty of the past," although his works also include hints of jazz, popular music (especially rhythm), and, occasionally, serialism. Ridout taught at the Toronto Conservatory and at the University of Toronto for many years, and his students have held prominent positions in the Canadian music world. Ridout was also a perceptive writer on music (Olnick 1992, 1130–31).

52 Louis Applebaum (1918–2000) grew up in Toronto and attended the University of Toronto, but also studied in New York. His primary interest was in composition for film and the theatre, but he also wrote for orchestra, choir, piano, wind band, and chamber ensembles. He wrote more than 250 film scores for the National Film Board and dozens of scores for CBC radio and television productions. He is perhaps best known for his long association with the Stratford Festival, where he served as both an administrator and composer of incidental music. Applebaum was also an arts administrator, working for the CBC, the National Arts Centre, the Canada Council, the Ontario Arts Council, and numerous other cultural agencies (Winters 1992, 31–32).

Notes to Part One Introduction

1 For example, the song *Farewell*, written in early 1898, incorporates the sudden shifts in tonality that are characteristic of his music throughout his career (Clarke 1983, 262)

2 Between 1902 and about 1904 Willan conducted Mendelssohn's *Lobgesang* and *St. Paul,* Elgar's *The Banner of St. George* and *Caractacus,* Handel's *Messiah,* and Coleridge-Taylor's *Song of Hiawatha,* among other works (Clarke 1983, 10–11).

3   Reginald Stewart (1900–1984) was born in Edinburgh and received instruction there, in Toronto, and in Paris. He was accomplished as both conductor and pianist, conducting throughout Canada and the United States and appearing as soloist with major orchestras, including the New York Philharmonic and the Chicago Symphony. In Toronto, he founded the Toronto Bach Choir and was music director during the 1930s of the Canadian Industries Ltd.'s radio broadcasts called *Opera House of the Air*. During the 1940s he lived mostly in the United States, where he conducted the Baltimore Symphony and was director of the Peabody Conservatory. He visited Canada to conduct at Stratford and on CBC. In 1962, he moved to Santa Barbara, California (Drynan 1992, 1252).

Notes to Chapter 1

1   According to the famous story, after hearing the Vincent Youmans song "Tea for Two," the conductor Nikolai Malko challenged Shostakovich to complete an orchestration of the tune in one hour. Shostakovich accepted the challenge and completed the piece in about forty-five minutes (Kennedy 1985, 724). One wonders if the challenge presented to Willan was to write the shortest possible complete composition.
2   Willan would reuse this melody as the secondary theme of the third movement of Symphony No. 1 (Clarke 1983, 94).
3   The term "fingerprint" is frequently used to identify musical constructs and principles that define a composer's individual approach to musical style. In Willan's case, Clarke and others have recognized a number of elements that recur throughout his oeuvre: gracious, singable melodies; a preference for uneven phrase lengths; tonalities that wander through many key areas without settling into any one; modal inflection; streams of parallel sixth chords; and "mystical choruses usually [consisting of] minor chords of a striking chromatic relationship to one another" (Clarke 1983, 262). In this study, it has also been observed that brass chorales functioning as structural articulations appear to be a fingerprint in Willan's orchestral music.
4   Bar 1 of this theme is, in fact, an inversion of bars 11 and 12 of theme 1A.
5   Ridout's score is not simply an orchestration of Willan's work. Ridout lists the piece as "revised and orchestrated"; he added several sections, smoothed out transitions, and did not always precisely follow Willan's scoring cues. Nonetheless, the new version is very effective and illustrates Ridout's skill as an orchestrator. Willan undoubtedly would have been pleased. While both Bryant and Clarke list this orchestration as from 1980, Ridout's score actually says 1979.

6   In his orchestration, Ridout set this accompaniment for harp and *pizzicato* double bass.
7   A similar technique will be seen in the analysis of *Coronation March* later in this study.
8   In this study, such passages will be labelled the "Willan rush."
9   The "Willan rush" and this melodic idea reappeared a number of years later in the third movement of Symphony No. 1.
10 As noted earlier, Willan apparently thought so as well. He reused a substantial amount of the musical material from this work in the finale of his Symphony No. 1.
11 The "Scotch snap" or "Lombard rhythm" is an inverted dotted rhythm in which an accented short note precedes the longer dotted note ($\flat \, \flat.$). It occurs frequently in Scottish folk music (perhaps related to traditional modes of bagpipe playing), and was a common rhythmic element of seventeenth-century music in Lombardy (Apel 1972, 243). Hungarian folk music also employs this rhythm to match the tune to the words. Many Hungarian words begin with short, accented syllables.
12 During this time, Willan also worked on three pieces for piano and orchestra. These pieces will be discussed later in this study.
13 Bryant's catalogue also identifies a sketch entitled *Darest Thou Now O Soul, Walk Out with Me toward the Unknown Region*, HWC 91 (Bryant 1972, 45). It is not at all clear from the surviving fragment that this work was intended for orchestra. In fact, the only connection to the orchestra is a single scoring cue designating one part for "trp," presumably trumpet.

Notes to Chapter 2

1   In the original production, the Overture led directly into the first scene of the play, without a clear-cut cadence. Clarke observes that the first act concludes with exactly the same music as the Overture, but with a conventional cadence. In concert performances, the final few bars of act 1 could easily be interpolated into the Overture to provide a convincing ending (Clarke 1983, 148–49).
2   Call number: Mus 1, 1969-1, III, 2
3   The chord on the downbeat in bar 3 is comprised of two simultaneous tritones!
4   The story behind the curious title is as follows: Willan and Napier Moore planned to write a comic opera, but Moore died before the project could begin. Willan, however, with his usual concentrated work ethic, had already composed the overture by the time of Moore's death, and thus the

piece exists today as an overture without an associated dramatic work (Clarke 1983, 112).
5   This tune first appeared in Willan's unfinished orchestral work *From the Highlands* of 1911 (Clarke 1983, 112).
6   The tritone progression (E-flat major to A major), which sounds so surprising here, will recur in other compositions reviewed in this study, and in other works by Willan.

Notes to Chapter 3

1   Bryant's catalogue lists a Scherzo in B Minor, HWC 75, for strings that Willan arranged in 1943–44 from the second movement of the *Miniature Suite for Organ*, HWC 148, of 1910. The arrangement was performed in Toronto, conducted by Godfrey Ridout (Bryant 1972, 42), but the score seems to have been lost.
2   King George and Queen Elizabeth were crowned on May 12, 1937 (Cannon 2009, 181).
3   In fact, this work does not settle into B-flat major, the apparent tonic, until bar 155.
4   Recalling the first strain at this point in the form was not unprecedented. Elgar had followed this procedure in *Pomp and Circumstance March No. 1*.
5   The score at this point specifies "Bells." Willan was obviously thinking of tubular bells or chimes, not glockenspiel, or what is generally known as "orchestra bells" in North America.
6   Clarke observes that this dedication probably was inspired by Elgar's dedication in his 1916 *Spirit of England*: "I dedicate to the memory of our glorious men, with a special thought for the Worcesters" (Clarke 1983, 110).
7   Clarke suggests that this tune may have its origins in English folk song (Clarke 1983, 110).
8   Willan apparently was fond of this poem. He set the complete poem as a song for voice and piano, which was published in the *Healey Willan Song Album No. 2* (Frederick Harris Music) in 1926. There is no musical connection between the song and *Poem*.
9   Heinz Unger (1895–1965) was born and trained in Berlin. He initially studied law, but in 1915 heard a performance of Gustav Mahler's *The Song of the Earth* and immediately decided to become a conductor and a Mahler specialist. Between 1919 and 1933 he conducted several of Berlin's most prominent musical organizations, including the Berlin Philharmonic. After moving to London in 1933, he guest-conducted many of the major

British orchestras. He appeared with the Toronto Symphony in 1937 and 1938, and moved to Toronto in 1948. In the following years, he conducted orchestras across Canada, especially those of the CBC. His lifelong fascination with the music of Mahler led to his conducting the Canadian premieres of many of that composer's works and to his receiving a number of awards from international Mahler societies. The York Concert Society was founded in 1953 especially as a showcase for his talents. The orchestras assembled by this organization included the best players resident in Toronto. Although Unger's programs tended to focus on the Austro-German repertoire, he also included compositions by Canadian composers (including Willan). He died of a heart attack in 1965 (Kallmann 1992, 1328–29).

10   This information was provided to the author by Captain Adams in interviews at his home in St. Catharines, Ontario, on April 20 and May 11, 2004. The unusual circumstances surrounding Adams's transcription will be discussed in detail later in this study.
11   This passage is repeated transposed down a perfect fourth at bars 45–46.
12   Lynnwood Farnam (1885–1930) was born and educated in Quebec. In 1900, he went to the Royal College of Music, London, on a three-year scholarship, which was extended by the College based on the excellence of his work. One of his teachers was W.S Hoyte, who had been Willan's teacher a few years earlier. He returned to Montreal in 1904 as a church organist, teacher, and recitalist. In 1913, he won the organist position at Emmanuel Church, Boston, and began building an international career. From 1919 until his death, he held prestigious organist positions in New York. When he was appointed to the Church of the Holy Communion, New York, in 1920, he had already given more than 500 recitals. A renowned teacher, he was invited to head the organ department at the Curtis Institute, Philadelphia, in 1927. Farnam's reputation was international. He gave numerous recitals in Europe on some of the world's greatest organs and was a universally admired interpreter of all of the organ literature, traditional and modern. His championing of Willan's Introduction, Passacaglia and Fugue undoubtedly lead to its wide acceptance as a masterpiece. His death at age forty-five from liver cancer was unexpected (Hawke 1992, 439).
13   The published version carries the dedication "In memory of a great artist, a valued friend and fellow-student."
14   Other writers have commented that the opening motive of this theme and others in Willan's oeuvre seem to hearken back to the chimes of Big Ben in London.

15 The published version for organ alone employs the key signature of D-flat major.
16 Willan, of course, had already written a work with organ as an orchestral instrument—*Epilogue*, composed in 1909, which, as noted earlier, may still be awaiting its premiere.

Notes to Chapter 4

1 This number is problematic. In the original (1972) catalogue Bryant assigned it to the unfinished *Overture* (with the Whitman quotation, "Know'st thou the excellent joys of youth"), which was reviewed earlier in this book. He used it again in the supplement to the catalogue (1982) to identify this fragment of an apparent piano concerto. The two works have no musical connection.
2 Brahms used the title *Ballade* for a group of descriptive piano works written in 1854 (Slonimsky 1992, 232).
3 In this context, the B-flat major chord seems to be functioning as a Neapolitan of the dominant, a highly coloured harmony that appears only at this point in the work.
4 The score indicates that Willan first placed this melody in the cellos but crossed it out and transferred it to horn.
5 Clarke notes that the primary theme of Liszt's Piano Concerto No. 1 in E-flat also has a prominent motive of three descending semitones and suggests that Liszt's Concerto may have influenced Willan (Clarke 1983, 103).
6 This is by no means the first time a new theme has appeared in the Development of a sonata-allegro form movement. Probably the most famous example is the first movement of Haydn's Symphony No. 45 ("Farewell").
7 Perhaps events like this are what Reginald Stewart meant when he claimed that Willan had an "innate instinct" for orchestration (Clarke 1983, 273).
8 Identifiers 1P, 1S, etc., will be used in the analysis of this movement to avoid confusion with the first movement (P1, S1, etc.).
9 Clarke identifies six secondary motives (Clarke 1983, 105). In this analysis, three of Clarke's motives are considered derivations of 1P and 2S.

Notes to Chapter 5

1 Calixa Lavallée (1842–1891) is best remembered as the composer of "O Canada." A supremely talented individual, he taught himself to play piano, organ, violin, and cornet; by age eleven he was playing organ at Notre-Dame Church in Montreal. His talent attracted the attention of a wealthy butcher,

Léon Derome, who became his lifelong patron. In 1857 he moved to New Orleans, where his abilities were recognized, most notably by a Spanish violinist named Olivera, who engaged him as accompanist for an extensive tour of Central and South America. Lavallée joined the Union Army as a musician during the American Civil War. Discharged in 1862, he returned to Canada, but found few opportunities and soon returned to the US. In 1870, he was appointed music director and superintendent of the Grand Opera House, an operatic and variety theatre in New York. His operetta *Loulou* was scheduled for performance in 1872, but the entire organization collapsed when its owner, James Fisk, was murdered. Lavallée returned to Montreal. A public subscription allowed him to go to Paris to study for two years, during which time his piano study *Le Papillon* was adopted by the Paris Conservatory and achieved international standing, and an orchestral suite was supposedly performed under a prominent Parisian conductor. Back in Quebec, he worked intensively to establish a national music conservatory and improve the quality of performance. Frustrated by the lack of interest, he moved permanently to the US in 1882. His reputation as pianist, conductor, and composer of light opera soon became national in scope, but he never ceased to work for his native country as well. He died in Boston, and his body was returned to Canada in 1933 (Potvin 1992, 727–29).

2 Percival Price (1901–1985) is primarily remembered as a carillonneur. The instrument commanded his attention during a trip to the Low Countries in 1921, and the same year he was appointed carillonneur at Metropolitan Church in Toronto. In 1925, he took up a similar position in New York and continued intensive studies abroad in carillon playing, conducting, and composition. In 1932–33, during studies in Vienna, he composed his symphony *The St. Lawrence*, which subsequently had two performances in Toronto: by Douglas Clark leading the Promenade Orchestra, and by the Toronto Symphony conducted by the composer. He had submitted his symphony to the University of Toronto as a doctoral exercise but it was rejected. He was engaged in 1927 to design the Peace Tower carillon in Ottawa and held the position of Dominion Carillonneur until 1939, when he joined the faculty of the University of Michigan, where he remained until his retirement in 1972. A ceaseless promoter of the carillon, he took its performance far beyond what had previously existed, extended its repertoire, and provided both music and literature to raise awareness of its possibilities (Barnwell 1992, 1076–77).

3 Clarence Lucas (1866–1947) was born in the Niagara Region but grew up mostly in Montreal. He began his career as conductor, trombonist,

violinist, and organist with a number of Montreal organizations, but moved to London and then to Paris to study. In 1888, he was appointed instructor of harmony and counterpoint at the Toronto College of Music. He left Canada permanently in 1890, moving first to Utica, New York, then to London. In London, he worked as a proofreader for Chappell Publishing, taught privately, wrote music journalism, and conducted. In the early 1900s he moved to New York, where he arranged and conducted Grieg's incidental music to *Peer Gynt* for its US premiere in 1906, and then toured the production throughout the US. Subsequently he returned to New York conducting musicals for George M. Cohan, writing music journalism, and composing songs and keyboard works. After 1919, he moved back and forth between London and Sèvres, France, where he died in 1947 (Hall 1992, 777–78).

4 This Dominion Day performance also included the premiere of Willan's *Coronation March (Marche solennelle)* (Clarke 1983, 33).

5 It was at this performance that Willan's former piano teacher, Evlyn Howard-Jones, played Brahms's Piano Concerto No. 2, and Willan got his picture in the Regina papers (Clarke 1983, 32).

6 These performances are listed on the flyleaf of Willan's own score, which is preserved in the National Library of Canada—Healey Willan Fonds, Mus 1, XXXIII, 1.

7 See, for example, the *Octet for Wind Instruments* of 1923.

8 This motive is an example of the harmonic analysis challenges presented by Willan's music. While the key signature and the first chord are B-flat major, an F-sharp minor triad is sustained throughout the introduction.

9 As noted earlier in relation to the Piano Concerto in C Minor, the labels 1M, 1P, etc., will be used in the analysis of this movement to avoid confusion with previous movements.

10 Other choices are certainly possible. As already seen, it is not unusual for Willan to recall primary material after the secondary area in his sonata-allegro forms. The recall of 2P at bar 112 could be an example of this procedure, and there is another arrival point at bar 117 that might mark the beginning of the Development. On the other hand, Willan returns to development of secondary area material at bar 117, which could suggest that he considered the Development to have begun at bar 88, at the point where he began the imitative development of the motive from the eleventh bar of the secondary theme.

11 Willan listed these performances on the flyleaf of his score, now owned by Berandol Music.

12 Susskind's performance in March 1958 was the result of the *Toronto Daily Star*'s charge that the Toronto Symphony was ignoring Symphony No. 2. Susskind thoroughly prepared the score, and Willan was pleased with his insights and attention to detail (Clarke 1983, 56).
13 Czech conductor Karel Ančerl (1908–1973) was trained in Prague and, as a proponent of modern repertoire, began conducting at contemporary festivals in his homeland and on Prague Radio. As a Jew, he was removed from his positions after the Nazis invaded in 1939. He was sent to the concentration camp at Theresienstadt and later to Auschwitz, where his entire family was put to death; by a fortuitous accident, he was spared. After the Second World War, he conducted most of Prague's primary musical organizations. In 1969, he was appointed conductor of the Toronto Symphony Orchestra and lived in Toronto until his death (Slonimsky 1992, 36).
14 Edmonton Symphony Orchestra, Uri Mayer, conductor, CBC Records, SMCD 5123.
15 The chord on the last beat of bar 3 is the "Tristan chord" and almost duplicates Wagner's voicing. It occurs again, transposed up a perfect fifth at the same point in the second phrase (bar 10). Since the contexts are so different, Willan probably was unaware that he had replicated this famous sonority.
16 This attention to orchestral colour may, of course, also be the influence of suggestions on scoring provided by Ettore Mazzoleni.
17 It is surely a coincidence that in 1957 when the *Toronto Daily Star* charged the Toronto Symphony of ignoring Willan's symphony, it recommended that Willan's work be performed instead of another presentation of the Tchaikovsky fifth symphony (Clarke 1983, 56).
18 During this presentation of P2, Willan engages in shifting metre to a much greater extent than in any other work in this study. Between bars 67 and 71, the metre changes four times: two bars of 3/2, one bar of 4/4, one bar of 5/4, and one bar of 3/4. This pattern is repeated at bar 76.
19 Willan actually foreshadows the horn call in first violins a bar earlier (bar 143).
20 Willan inserted a similar "Development theme" in the first movement of the Piano Concerto in C Minor using a comparable organic approach.
21 Willan was sixty in the summer of 1941.
22 Similar short, loud chords appear often in Stravinsky's music, where they have the same function—separating phrases, subsections, and sections. Willan's use of this technique in Symphony No. 2 is subtler than Stravinsky's

but is similar enough to make us wonder about an influence. Certainly, by the mid-1930s many of Stravinsky's most popular compositions were well known, and the composer himself conducted *Firebird* and *Petrushka* with the Toronto Symphony in 1937 (Beckwith, 1992, 1302).

23 Clarke suggests that this is a sly reference to *The Sorcerer's Apprentice* (Clarke 1983, 99).

24 Beginning Development sections with the closing theme of the Exposition is not a particularly unusual procedure. Mozart, for example, took this approach in some of his symphonies.

25 Clarke identifies this bar as the beginning of the Recapitulation (Clarke 1983, 101).

Note to Part Two Introduction

1 Boosey and Hawkes, the copyright holder, has assured the author that it intends to release a new printing, but as of the time of writing it has not appeared.

Notes to Chapter 6

1 The dedication in the printed score reads: "This composition derives its title from Royce Hall, the concert auditorium on the Los Angeles campus of the University of California, where it was first performed. It is dedicated to Mr. Patton McNaughton, conductor of the U.C.L.A. Band."

2 Howard Cable (b. 1920) was born and educated in Toronto. In the 1930s he was a student at the Toronto Conservatory (one of his teachers was Healey Willan) and graduated in 1939 with an Associateship in conducting and bandmastership. While a student he began working in radio, which led to a long career as conductor-arranger-composer for the CBC. He established his own concert band in the early 1950s using many of Toronto's finest wind players. In the mid-1960s he worked as conductor and arranger on Broadway. Cable has been associated with most of the principal arts festivals and organizations in Canada over his long career, including the Banff Festival, the Charlottetown Festival, the CNE Grandstand, the Canadian Brass. He has served as pops conductor for a number of Canadian orchestras, often performing his own arrangements. His original compositions include works on Canadian folk songs in several genres, incidental music to dramatic productions, a children's opera, a musical, among others. He has received an honorary doctorate from the University of Lethbridge and an award from the Canadian Band Directors Association in recognition of

his contribution to band music at all levels (Kallmann, Potvin, and Winters 1992, 182–83).

3 William Teague has become something of a mystery to Canadian band conductors, who have often wondered who he was and why he was selected to score *Royce Hall Suite*. Fortunately, the Willan archive in the National Library of Canada holds several letters that provide the identifying information included in this study.

4 Teague's arrangements were published by a number of companies, including Remick Music, T.B. Harms, and M. Witmark and Sons. All of these companies were imprints owned after 1929 by Warner Bros. Publications. BMI was one of the names of the Warner Bros. publishing empire, so Teague would have been well known to BMI executives. See website of Warner-Chappell Music: www.warnerchappell.com (accessed March 29, 2004).

5 Healey Willan Fonds, National Library of Canada, box 143, BMI Canada folder.

6 Curiously, another American musician named William Teague was active and well known at the same time. Dr. William C. Teague was the long-time organist and choir director at St. Mark's Episcopal Church and Professor of Music at Centenary College in Shreveport, Louisiana. He had an international reputation as an organist and conductor. Dr. Teague and Willan were good friends. Teague regularly programmed Willan's organ music on his international tours and recorded the Introduction, Passacaglia and Fugue.

On at least one occasion, Dr. Teague was confused with his namesake. He was engaged to conduct the New Orleans Symphony, and was mistaken by the band director at Tulane University as the arranger of *Royce Hall Suite*. He was wined and dined, but was quite embarrassed when it became apparent that a mistake had been made (personal correspondence between Dr. William C. Teague and the author, March 10, 2004).

7 Healey Willan Fonds, National Library of Canada, box 143, BMI Canada folder.

8 The Goldman Band of New York was founded in 1911 by Edwin Franko Goldman (1878–1956), a cornet player and a well-trained musician (he studied composition with Dvořák). In 1918, the band began giving a series of outdoor summer concerts in New York, first at Columbia University, later on the Mall in Central Park, a tradition which continued for more than six decades. In 1937, Edwin's son, Richard Franko Goldman (1910–1980), began assisting his father with the organization and

conducting of the band. Richard took over conducting the band in the early 1950s and continued until ill health required him to step down in 1979. Although the band continued for a few more years under different conductors and names, the Goldman Band essentially dissolved with Richard's retirement.

The Goldman Band was exceptional for its longevity, professionalism, and musicality. Its members were many of New York's most accomplished musicians, and, indeed, they needed to be first-rate professionals. The summer season consisted of some sixty concerts, and the band prided itself on never repeating a single program. The Goldmans were accomplished musicians whose intention for their band was to perform music of the highest quality with the same artistic excellence that would be found at symphony orchestra concerts. The Goldman Band's precision, accuracy, and expressivity were exceptional in its early years and provided a model for many other ensembles that developed during and after its long tenure. The Goldmans were also committed to improving the literature available to bands. They restored to the repertoire a number of eighteenth- and nineteenth-century compositions that had been "lost," and they actively commissioned established composers. Many of the original works now considered to be core repertoire were written for the Goldman Band (Goldman 1946, 77–80; Slonimsky 1992, 644).

9   The third page of this document is not on letterhead and is not in Willan's hand. It consists of a series of brief comments ("cleff [sic] signs, "dynamics," etc.) that are apparently reminders written on a separate piece of paper by Teague during the process of the scoring.

10 This is apparently an error. The section referred to begins at measure 23, not 26.

11 Charles O'Neill (1882–1964) was born in Scotland and trained in Glasgow and London. By his teenage years he was an accomplished organist and cornetist. He moved to the United States in 1901 and to Canada in 1905, where he became the cornet soloist with the Royal Canadian Horse Artillery Band based in Kingston, Ontario. Shortly afterwards, the Defence Department sent him to Kneller Hall in England to train as a band director. On his return to Canada in 1910, he developed military bands in Quebec City to a very high level. He also continued his study, becoming one of the first music graduates of McGill University. O'Neill came to international attention through his association with the Canadian National Exhibition band festival and the CBC. His reputation was especially recognized in the

US—he counted John Phillip Sousa and Edwin Franko Goldman among his friends. In 1937, O'Neill left military service and took up a series of important teaching positions in the United States and Canada, including the Royal Conservatory of Music, Toronto, from 1948 to 1954 (Kallmann/ Plouffe 1992, 964). Considering his stellar reputation as a band director and the fact that he was teaching in Toronto, it is hardly surprising that Willan would have solicited his opinion on *Royce Hall Suite*.

12 Healey Willan Fonds, National Library of Canada, box 37, Royce Hall Suite.
13 This famous band was formed in 1872 and continues to exist today. Justly celebrated for its spectacular technical prowess and accomplished musicianship, it has had a long series of distinguished conductors, and many important French composers have written music for its use. Perhaps the best known Garde Républicaine commission is Florent Schmitt's *Dionysiaques*, a very challenging composition that is now established in the core repertoire (Goldman 1946, 67).
14 Robert Rosevear (1915–2012) was born and trained in the United States. In 1946 he joined the Faculty of Music, University of Toronto, and remained there until his retirement in 1978. At Toronto, he developed a program for the training of future music teachers that became the model for similar programs at other Canadian universities. He was the first chairman of the Music Education Department at the University of Toronto, founded both the Royal Conservatory Concert Band and the University of Toronto Concert Band, and conducted the University of Toronto Symphony Orchestra for six seasons. His writings, lectures, clinics, and adjudications set an important standard for Canadian instrumental music education. After his retirement, he moved to Florida, but continued to work for the improvement of music education (Shand 1992, 1148).
15 Healey Willan Fonds, National Library of Canada, box 143, Associated folder.
16 Willan's holograph score names this movement Introduction and Fugue.
17 *Harmoniemusik* refers to small wind bands (most commonly of six to ten players) that were very popular in European courts in the eighteenth and early nineteenth centuries. Most of the major composers of the time, as well as a great many lesser-known figures, contributed to the vast extant repertoire written for these ensembles.
18 Considering the influence of the fugue subject on melodic construction throughout this work, it seems likely that the fugue was the first music composed by Willan.
19 The second statement modulates briefly to C-flat major.

20 Hindemith, Symphony in B-flat; Schuller, *Symphony for Brass and Percussion*; Schuman, *George Washington Bridge*; Persichetti, *Divertimento for Band*; Piston, *Tunbridge Fair*; Mennin, *Canzona*.
21 William Thais Atkins (1907–1979) was born in England and trained as a bandmaster at Kneller Hall. Following a successful career in the British army, he moved to Toronto after the Second World War, and from 1947 to 1968 served as bandmaster of the Queen's Own Rifles Regimental Band. He also conducted the Brampton Citizens Band and was well known as teacher and adjudicator (Kopstein 1992, 55).
22 See Bryant 1975, 44; and Clarke 1983, 110.
23 Healey Willan Fonds, National Library of Canada, box 125, folder A, 1953–66.
24 St. Paul's has been the regimental church of the Queen's Own Rifles since 1910. See official website of the Queen's Own Rifles, http://www.qor.com (accessed April 2, 2009).
25 Atkins was referring to Willan's two brass fanfares commissioned by the Hudson's Bay Company for the "rent-paying" ceremony before Queen Elizabeth II in Winnipeg on July 24, 1959 (reviewed in detail later in this book).
26 Healey Willan Fonds, National Library of Canada, box 141, folder Wic-Woo.
27 He was probably referring to the massed band performance that is a regular occurrence in the evening of Canada Day, July 1.
28 Healey Willan Fonds, National Library of Canada, box 125, folder A, 1953–66.
29 Interestingly, Atkins's letter, which is handwritten and undated, closes with the words: "With every good wish to Mrs. Willan and yourself." Atkins was apparently unaware that Gladys Willan had died in December 1964.
30 Willan seems to have liked the idea of a fanfare comprised of root-position triads as a linking device, especially in ceremonial works. At least four other compositions employ this technique (Clarke 1983, 109).
31 This work was reviewed in the orchestral section of this study under the title *Centennial (or Ceremonial) March* (Willan's autograph score displays both titles). To distinguish the concert band version reviewed here from the orchestral version, the author combined both titles in a manner that clearly illustrates the work's purpose and adheres to the composer's intent.
32 The band's schedule included: daily performances for the changing of the guard on Parliament Hill in the morning; playing for departing dignitaries

at Uplands Airport at 1 p.m. and for arriving dignitaries in front of the eternal flame on Parliament Hill at 4 p.m.; as well as regular concerts and participation in special events, civilian and military, associated with the centennial celebrations. Interview with Captain Charles Adams, May 11, 2004.

33   Charles Adams was born in England in 1916, but grew up in St. Catharines, Ontario. As a young man he played trombone in military and community bands in the Niagara area, but when he joined the Canadian Army he was trained as an artillery sergeant. In the early 1950s he switched trades to become a musician, and in 1954 was sent by the Canadian Army to Kneller Hall in England to train as a bandmaster. He completed his training in 1957 and was immediately assigned to the Royal Canadian Corps of Signals Band in Lahr, Germany, where he developed a fine ensemble. He became bandmaster of the Canadian Guards Band at Camp Petawawa in 1966; however, that entire regiment was reduced to zero strength with the unification of the Canadian Forces in 1968. Adams retired from the military and taught high school for a number of years in the Ottawa Valley. After his retirement from teaching, he returned to his hometown, St. Catharines, Ontario. Interview with Captain Charles Adams, May 11, 2004.

34   In 2004, Adams completed a full score. Copies of this full score and complete sets of parts are now housed in the National Library of Canada, Ottawa, and in the Canadian Music Centre, Toronto.

35   This information was provided by Captain Charles Adams in interviews with the author on April 20 and May 11, 2004. Both Bryant (Bryant 1972, 44) and Clarke (Clarke 1983, 66) list the performers as the Grenadier Guards Band of Montreal. Captain Adams assured the author that the band was the Canadian Guards.

36   Captain Adams was scheduled to conduct this performance. He visited McMaster and rehearsed his transcription with the band—he was eighty-eight years old and hadn't conducted for some twenty years. The McMaster students were amazed by his vitality and commitment to the music. Unfortunately, he became ill a few days before the performance and, to the great disappointment of everyone in the band, was unable to appear on the concert.

37   Willan also scored the antecedent of this third appearance of theme one for trumpets, a quite dramatic contrast to the earlier woodwind statements.

38   Adams's use of the *Dal segno* in his transcription shows how thoroughly he analyzed the music, and probably also indicates the pressure he was under

to complete his score in the short time available to him. The written-in repeat saved him a lot of writing.

39 Adams added the directive *Largamente* at the beginning of the Coda, and, while it does not appear in Willan's score, it is well suited to the character of the music.

40 It is important to note that Adams was working from a full score, while Teague and Atkins had to contend with short scores mostly on two staves.

Notes to Chapter 8

1 This fanfare was performed as a flourish at the installation of Dr. Patrick Dean as president of McMaster University on November 19, 2010.

2 George Maybee (1913–1973), organist, choir director, educator, was one of Willan's students in Toronto and a long-time friend. He took additional training in England in organ and church music. His most prominent position was organist and choirmaster at St. George's Cathedral in Kingston, Ontario, where he developed an outstanding men and boys choir, which toured Britain in 1954 and 1965, and was the first overseas choir to sing regular services at Westminster Abbey, St. Paul's Cathedral, and other important churches. They also toured North America and gave a concert in Washington, DC, in November 1964 honouring the late President John F. Kennedy. A successful high school teacher, Maybee also lectured at Queen's University. He is credited with improving the choral singing standards in Canada and the US (Whittingham 1992, 822).

3 The ceremony took place in 1949, but, according to Maybee, the music was written in 1948.

4 Healey Willan Fonds, Correspondence, box 135, folder "George N. Maybee."

5 This final ceremony (1970) was the site of a hilarious occurrence. The Hudson's Bay Company (HBC) decided that, for this occasion, live beavers would be offered. When the Queen attempted to accept the emblematic "rent," the beavers began to fight and then to copulate. Surprised, the Queen demanded: "Whatever are they doing?" Lord Amory, the HBC governor and supervisor of the event, replied: "Ma'am, it's no good asking me. I'm a bachelor." The Queen quickly recovered her composure and coolly responded: "I *quite* understand" (Newman 1985, 90–91).

6 A letter dated May 7, 1959, from F.B. Walker, executive assistant at the Hudson's Bay Company, to Will Croombs of Boosey & Hawkes (Canada)

Ltd., requested the loan of eight fanfare trumpets. Hudson's Archives, Winnipeg, HBCA RG2/8/785-792. Apparently, Boosey & Hawkes complied with this request, and, indeed, it seems unlikely they would have refused, considering the royal presence and the solemnity of the occasion.

7 All of the background information included in this section has been gleaned from letters between Walker and Mazzoleni, which are preserved in the Hudson's Bay Archives, HBCA RG2/8/785-792.

8 By May 15, the Hudson's Bay Company (HBC) had secured permission from the Department of National Defence to use musicians from the Royal Canadian Air Force Band stationed in Edmonton. The "professionally copied parts" are conserved in the HBC Archives.

9 Flight Lieutenant Carl Friberg, Deputy Commander, RCAF Band, Edmonton.

10 The mention of E-flat trumpet is further confirmation that Fanfares 2 and 3 of the set catalogued by Bryant as HWC 81 were those written for the "rent paying" ceremony in Winnipeg.

11 The only comment in the press appears to have been by the *Winnipeg Free Press*, which, in its front-page story on the ceremony published on July 24, 1959, mentions that "eight trumpeters and a timpanist from the Royal Canadian Air Force Band of Edmonton played fanfares written for the occasion by Canadian composer Dr. Healey Willan."

12 For example, this progression is duplicated in bars 32–33 of the fifth movement, "The Magi," of the Christmas cantata *The Mystery of Bethlehem* (1923), and in the final cadential bars of *Overture to an Unwritten Comedy* (1951). It sounds equally surprising in the harmonic context of both works.

13 As will be seen later, this was probably William Atkins, the conductor of the band of the Queen's Own Rifles.

14 Interestingly, in the existing set of three fanfares, this piece is titled simply Fanfare No. 1, while the other two are designated as "Ceremonial" fanfares.

15 Healey Willan Fonds, 1969-1, XXXVII, 7.

16 Healey Willan Fonds, National Library of Canada, box 141, folder Wic-Woo.

17 Healey Willan Fonds, National Library of Canada, box 125, folder A, 1953–66. Apparently, then, the score currently in the Willan archive is that written out by Atkins. Why this was necessary, since he must have had a score in order to perform them in May 1960, is unclear, unless Willan's original was a short score.

18 Healey Willan Fonds, National Library of Canada, box 133, folder L.
19 The two Ceremonial fanfares were played, probably for the first time since 1962, on November 20, 2011, by the brass section of McMaster University Concert Band, conducted by the author.

Notes to Conclusion

1 To date, only three of Willan's orchestral works have been released in professional, commercial pressings:
   - Symphony No. 2, Edmonton Symphony Orchestra, Uri Mayer, cond., CBC, SMCD 5123, 1993;
   - Piano Concerto in C Minor, Toronto Symphony Orchestra, Mario Bernardi, cond., Arthur Ozolins, piano, CBC, SMCD 5108, 1991;
   - *Centennial (Ceremonial) March*, Edmonton Symphony Orchestra, Uri Mayer, cond., *Great Orchestral Marches*, CBC, SMCD 5093, 1990.
2 Music retailers have informed the author that, although this work has been out of print for some time, they still receive a number of requests for it every year.

Bibliography

Apel, Willi, ed. 1972. *Harvard Dictionary of Music*. 2nd ed. Cambridge, MA: Belknap Press of Harvard University Press.

Barnwell, F. Michael. 1992. "Price, (Frank) Percival." In *Encyclopedia of Music in Canada*, 1076–77.

Beckwith, John. 1992. "MacMillan, Sir Ernest (Alexander Campbell)" and "Toronto Symphony." In *Encyclopedia of Music in Canada*, 788–91, 1300–5.

———. 1997. *Music Papers: Articles and Talks by a Canadian Composer 1961–1994*. Ottawa: Golden Dog Press.

Bryant, Giles. 1972. *Healey Willan Catalogue*. Ottawa: National Library of Canada.

———. 1975. "Willan, Healey." In *Contemporary Canadian Composers*, edited by Keith MacMillan and John Beckwith, 238–42. Toronto: Oxford University Press.

———. 1982. *Healey Willan Catalogue: Supplement*. Ottawa: National Library of Canada.

Brown, Thomas C., and Giles Bryant. 1992. "Willan, (James) Healey." In *Encyclopedia of Music in Canada*, 2nd ed., edited by Helmut Kallmann, Giles Potvin, and Kenneth Winters, 1405–8. Toronto: University of Toronto Press.

Cannon, John, ed. 2009. *The Oxford Companion to British History*. 1st rev. ed. Oxford: Oxford University Press.

Clarke, F.R.C. 1983. *Healey Willan: Life and Music*. Toronto: University of Toronto Press.

Corvin, Maria. 1992. "Susskind (Süsskind), Walter." In *Encyclopedia of Music in Canada*, 1266.

Corvin, Maria, and Helen McNamara. 1992. "Agostini, Lucio." In *Encyclopedia of Music in Canada*, 8–9.

Drynan, Margaret. 1992. "Bryant, Giles" and "Stewart, Reginald (Drysdale)." In *Encyclopedia of Music in Canada*, 174–75 and 1252.

Eyk, Jason van, ed. 2010. "FRC Clarke 1931–2009." *Ontario Notations* 16, no. 1 (Winter 2010): 29.

Frere, W.H., et al, eds. 1909. *Hymns Ancient and Modern for Use in the Services of the Church with Accompanying Tunes*. London: William Clowes and Sons.

Goldman, Richard Franko. 1946. *The Concert Band*. New York and Toronto: Rinehart and Company.

Hall, Frederick A. 1992. "Butcher, Agnes." In *Encyclopedia of Music in Canada*, 180.

Hall, Sharyn Lea. 1992. "Lucas, Clarence (Reynolds)." In *Encyclopedia of Music in Canada*, 777–78.

Hawke, H. William. 1992. "Farnam, (Walter) Lynnwood." In *Encyclopedia of Music in Canada*, 439.

Kallmann, Helmut. 1960. *A History of Music in Canada 1534–1914*. Toronto: University of Toronto Press.

———. 1992. "Adaskin, John," "Unger, Heinz," "Waddington, Geoffrey" and "Willan (b. Hall), Gladys (Ellen)." In *Encyclopedia of Music in Canada*, 6, 1328–29, 1380, 1405. Kallmann, Helmut, and Hélène Plouffe. 1992. "O'Neill, Charles." In *Encyclopedia of Music in Canada*, 964.

Kallmann, Helmut, Carl Morey, and Patricia Wardrop. 1992. "Toronto." 1296.

Kallmann, Helmut, Giles Potvin, and Kenneth Winters, eds. 1992. *Encyclopedia of Music in Canada*, 2nd ed. Toronto: University of Toronto Press.

Kennedy, Michael. 1985. *The Oxford Dictionary of Music*. Oxford and New York: Oxford University Press.

Kopstein, Jack. 1992. "Atkins, William (Thais)." In *Encyclopedia of Music in Canada*, 55.

Lister, Rota Herzberg. 1988. "Coulter, John William." In *The Canadian Encyclopedia*, 2nd ed., 1: 525. Edmonton: Hurtig.

McClennan, William. 1986. "Moore, Earl Vincent." In *New Grove Dictionary of American Music*, edited by H. Wiley Hitchcock and Stanley Sadie, 3: 267–68. London: Macmillan.

McLean, Eric. 1992. "Clarke, Douglas (William)." In *Encyclopedia of Music in Canada*, 274. McLean, Maud. 1992. "Iseler, Elmer (Walter)." In *Encyclopedia of Music in Canada*, 638.

Newman, Peter C. 1985. *Company of Adventurers*. Vol. 1. Markham, ON: Penguin Canada.

Olnick, Harvey. 1992. "Ridout, Godfrey." In *Encyclopedia of Music in Canada*, 1130–31.

Pitman, Walter. 2008. *Elmer Iseler: Choral Visionary*. Toronto: Dundurn.
Potvin, Gilles. 1992. "Beaudet, Jean-Marie or Jean," "Lavallée, Calixa (Callixte)." In *Encyclopedia of Music in Canada*, 95–96, 727–29.
Reeves, Marjorie, and Jenyth Worsley. 2006. *Favourite Hymns: 2000 Years of Magnificat*. London and New York: Continuum.
Renwick, William. 1982. "The Contrapuntal Style of Healey Willan." Unpublished master of music thesis, University of British Columbia.
Richardson, Constance. 1951. "Evlyn Howard-Jones." In *Music and Letters* 32, no. 2 (April 1951): 198–99.
Ridout, Godfrey. 1992. "Mazzoleni, Ettore." In *Encyclopedia of Music in Canada*, 823.
Sadie, Stanley, ed. 1988. *The Norton/Grove Concise Encyclopedia of Music*. New York and London: W.W. Norton.
Searle, Humphrey. 1980. "Franz Liszt." In *The New Grove Dictionary of Music and Musicians*, edited by Stanley Sadie, 11: 28–74. London: Macmillan.
Seay, Albert. 1975. *Music in the Medieval World*. 2nd ed. Englewood Cliffs, NJ: Prentice-Hall.
Shand, Patricia. 1992. "Rosevear, Robert (Allan)." In *Encyclopedia of Music in Canada*, 1148.
Simpson, Robert 1967. *The Essence of Bruckner*. London: Victor Gollancz.
Slonimsky, Nicolas, ed. 1992. *Baker's Biographical Dictionary of Musicians*. 8th ed. New York: Schirmer.
Vaughan Williams, Ralph, and J.H. Arnold, eds. 1933. *The English Hymnal with Tunes*. London: Oxford University Press.
Whittingham, Anthony. 1992. "Maybee, George (Nelson)." In *Encyclopedia of Music in Canada*, 822.
Winters, Kenneth. 1992. "Applebaum, Louis." In *Encyclopedia of Music in Canada*, 31–32.

Index

Adams, Captain Charles A.W., xvii–xviii, 66, 139, 158–62, 197n10, 207n33, 207n35, 207n36, 207–8n38, 208n39, 208n40
Adaskin, John, 12, 43, 191n42
Agostini, Lucio, 9, 190n35
American Organist, 13–14
Ančerl, Karel, 111, 201n13
Anglo-Catholic Rite, 2, 4, 7, 185n6, 187n13, 188n22
Applebaum, Louis, 16, 193n52
Atkins, Capt William, 152–57, 178–79, 206n21, 206n25, 206n29, 208n40, 209n13, 209n17

Bach, Johann Sebastian, 7, 24
Band of the Canadian Guards, 66, 158, 206–7n32, 207n35
Bartók, Béla, 10, 77, 191n38
Bax, Arnold, 16, 20
Beaudet, Jean-Marie, 10, 77, 191n39
Beckenham: Church of St. George, 2
Beethoven, Ludwig van, 87
Berandol Music, xviii, 183–84, 190n33, 200n11
Boosey & Hawkes, 152–54, 182, 208–9n6
Boult, Sir Adrian, 12, 192n45

Brahms, Johannes: *Ballade*, 198n2; influence of, 9, 16, 74–75, 93, 187n11; orchestration, 21; Piano Concerto No. 2, 9, 200n5
British Broadcasting Corporation: broadcasts, 12; commissions, 12
Bruckner, Anton, 121
Brown, Thomas C., 1, 186n3
Bryant, Giles, 1, 15, 186n4, 194n5
Burgess, Francis, 4
Butcher, Agnes, 10, 77, 91, 191n38

Cable, Howard, 140, 202–3n2
Calvert, Morley: *Introduction and Scherzo*, 185n1
Canadian Broadcasting Corporation: broadcasts, 10–13, 15, 58; commissions, 9–10, 58–59, 192n44; CBC Montreal Orchestra, 10, 77; CBC Toronto Orchestra, 9–10, 12–13, 59, 111, 192n47; *Portrait of Healey Willan*, 14
Canadian Centennial, 14, 68, 157, 192n48
Canadian Federation of Music Teachers Association, 13
Canadian Music Centre: John Adaskin Project, xvi–xvii,

191n42; research and performance assistance, xvii, 138, 182–84, 191n42, 207n34
Canadian Opera Company, 15, 192n47
Charles II, 171–72
Clarke, Douglas, 9, 94, 189n2, 199n2
Clarke, F.R.C., 1, 20–21, 33, 42, 69, 78, 81, 93, 99–100, 104, 106, 110, 121, 127, 131, 134–35, 185n2, 194n5, 196n6, 196n7, 198n5, 202n23, 202n25
Coakley, Donald: *Songs for the Morning Band*, 185n1
Coleridge-Taylor, Samuel: *Song of Hiawatha*, 193n2
Colgrass, Michael: *Old Churches*, 185n1
Concordia Publishing House, xviii, 11
Copland, Aaron, 136
Coulter, John, 9–10, 190n34

Eastbourne: St. Saviour's Church, 2
Edmonton: Edmonton Symphony Orchestra, 111, 201n14, 210n1; Royal Canadian Air Force Band, 209n8, 209n11
Elgar, Edward: *Caractacus*, 193n2; *Enigma Variations*, 192n45; influence of, 16, 20, 43, 61, 132, 134; *Pomp and Circumstance March No. 1*, 48, 51, 61, 66, 68, 158, 160–61, 196n4; *Spirit of England*, 196n6; *The Banner of St. George*, 193n2
Elizabeth II, 12–13, 59–60
European American Music, xviii

Farnham, Lynnwood, 69–70, 197n12
Fellowes, Edmund Horace, 8, 189n24
Festival Singers of Canada, 186n3, 186n4, 193n50
Frederick Harris Co., 163, 188n16, 196n8
Freedman, Harry: *À la claire fontaine*, 185n1; *Blanche comme la neige*, 185n1
French Overture, 145
Friberg, Flight Lieutenant Carl, 173–74, 209n9

Garde Républicaine Band of Paris, 144, 205n13
George VI and Queen Elizabeth, 9, 47, 60, 196n2
Goldman Band of New York, 141, 203–4n8

Hamilton: McMaster University, xvii, 14, 158, 191n38, 208n1; McMaster University Concert Band, 158, 207n36, 210n19
Handel, George Frideric, 145, 147
Harmoniemusik, 147, 205n17
Harty, Hamilton: *Irish Symphony*, 30
Haydn, Franz Joseph: Symphony No. 45 "Farewell," 198n6
Heap, Margaret and Harry, 192n46
Hindemith, Paul: as composer, 151; Symphony in B-Flat, 206n20
Holst, Gustav, 43, 134, 164, 187n10, 192n45
Howard-Jones, Evlyn, 3, 9, 74, 187n11, 200n5
Hoyte, Dr. William Stevenson, 2–3, 187n10, 197n12

Hudson's Bay Company: archives, xvii, 171, 208–9n6, 209n7, 209n8; charter, 171–72; "Company of Adventurers," 171–72; tribute to English sovereigns, 13, 172–73, 177–78, 206n25, 208n5, 209n8; Walker F.B., 173–74, 208–9n6, 209n7

Iseler, Elmer, 15, 193n50

Jimmy mo mhíle stór, 29–30, 33–34

Kallmann, Helmut, 170
Kingston: Queen's University, 13, 185n2; Royal Canadian Horse Artillery Band, 204n11; St George's Cathedral, 11, 169, 208n2

Lavallée, Calixa, 93, 198–99n1
Lehmberg, Stanford E., 178–80
Library and Archives Canada (National Library of Canada), xvii–xviii, 25, 39, 73, 138, 141–42, 152, 169, 171, 176, 180, 182–84, 186n3, 186n4, 188n23, 189n27, 191n39, 200n6, 203n3, 203n5, 203n7, 205n12, 205n15, 206n23, 206n26, 206n28, 207n33, 208n4, 209n15, 209n16, 209n17, 210n18
Liszt, Franz: piano concertos, 78, 198n5; Sonata in B Minor, 78; "thematic transformation," 78
London: All Saints' Margaret Street, 3, 187n10; London Gregorian Association, 4; Queen's Hall, 20; Royal Academy of Music, 4, 187n10; Royal College of Music, 187n10, 197n12; St. John the Baptist Kensington, 4, 6, 20, 187n12; St. Paul's Cathedral, 4; Westminster Cathedral, 4, 187n14
Los Angeles (California): UCLA concert band, 139–40, 202n1; University of California, 11, 139, 202n1
"low Anglican," 6
Lucas, Clarence, 94, 199–200n3

MacMillan, Sir Ernest, 8–11, 111, 189n25, 192n47
Maybee, George, 170, 208n2
Mayer, Uri, 111
Mazzoleni, Ettore, 9–10, 21, 77, 111, 173–75, 190n31, 190n36, 201n16, 209n7
McNaughton, Patton, 139–40, 202n1
Mendelssohn-Bartholdy, Felix, 3: *Lobegesang*, 3, 193n2; *St. Paul*, 3, 193n2
Mennin, Peter: as composer, 151; *Canzona*, 206n20
Montreal: Church of St. Andrew and St. Paul, 6; Montreal Symphony Orchestra, 9, 94, 189n28
Moore, Napier, 195–96n4
Mozart, Wolfgang Amadeus, 202n24

National Film Board of Canada: *Man of Music*, 13, 65

O'Neill, Captain Charles, 142–44, 204–5n11
O'Sullivan, Denis, 29–30
Ottawa: Centennial Centre, 15, 158; National Arts Centre, 191n39; Parliament Hill, 14, 66, 157–58

Oxford University Press, 11, 14

Parry, Sir Hubert, 3, 16, 20
Persichetti, Vincent: composer, 151; *Divertimento for Band*, 206n21
Peters, C.F., xviii, 11
Piston, Walter: as composer 151; *Tunbridge Fair*, 206n21
Price, Percival: *The St. Lawrence*, 94, 199n2

Queen's Own Rifles, 10, 55,152–53, 157, 178–79, 206n22, 206n25, 209n13

Rheinberger, Josef, Concerto No. 1 in F, 3
Ridout, Godfrey, 16, 21, 29, 34, 55, 57, 193n51, 194n5, 195n6, 196n1
Riegger, Wallingford, 136
Rosevear, Robert, 144, 152, 205n14
Royal Canadian College of Organists, 13
Royal College of Organists (England), 13

Schuller, Gunther: as composer, 130, 151; *Symphony for Brass and Percussion*, 206n21
Schuman, William: as composer, 136, 151; *George Washington Bridge*, 206n21
Shostakovich, Dimitri: *Tahiti Trot*, 24, 194n1
St. Albans: life in, 2; St. Saviour's, 3; St. Cecelia Choir, 3
Stanford, Charles Villiers, 16, 20
Stewart, Reginald, 21, 47, 94, 194n3, 198n 7

Stravinsky, Igor, 97, 130, 200n7, 201–2n22
Sullivan, Sir Arthur: as composer, 3–4; *The Pirates of Penzance*, 3
Susskind, Walter, 13, 21, 111, 192n47, 201n12

Tchaikovsky, Pyotr, Symphony No. 5, 13, 114, 130, 201n18;
Teague, Dr. William C., 203n6
Teague, William, 140–44, 182, 203n4, 203n5, 204n9, 208n42
Terry, Sir Richard, 4, 187n14
Toronto: Arts and Letters Club, 6, 188n19; Church of St. Mary Magdalene, 7–8, 12–13, 15, 186n4, 188n22; Eaton Auditorium, 62; Maple Leaf Gardens, 144; O'Keefe Centre, 15; Royal Conservatory of Music, 185n1, 186n4, 204–5n11, 205n14; Royal Conservatory Opera School, 190n31; Royal Conservatory Symphony Orchestra, 111; St. Paul's Bloor Street, 5–7, 11, 13–15, 152–53, 157, 206n25; Toronto Conservatory, 1, 5–6, 8, 77, 190n31, 190n32, 193n51, 202–3n2; Toronto Conservatory Orchestra, 9–10; *Toronto Daily Star*, 13, 201n12; Toronto Mendelssohn Choir, 6–7, 10, 189n25, 192n47, 193n50; Toronto Promenade Symphony Orchestra, 47, 94, 199n2; Toronto Symphony Orchestra, 9–11, 13, 77, 111, 189n25, 190n31, 190n32, 191n42, 192n47, 199n2, 201n12, 201n13, 201–2n23, 210n1; University of Toronto, 1, 6, 8, 11, 15, 138, 186n4,

193n51; University of Toronto Concert Band, 144, 152, 205n14; University of Toronto Faculty of Music, 8, 15–16, 141, 173, 205n14; University Player's Club at Hart House, 7; York Concert Society Orchestra, 62, 196–97n9

Unger, Heinz, 62, 196–97n9
University of Michigan, 9, 199n2
Urbs beata Hierusalem, 25

Vaughan Williams, Ralph, 131

Waddington, Geoffrey, 9, 59, 111, 190n32
Wanstead: life in, 3, 20; Wanstead Choral Society, 3, 20
Willan, Bernard, 10, 55, 152
Willan, Eleanor (Healey), 2
Willan, Gladys Ellen (Hall): 4, 14, 188n16, 206n29
Willan, Healey: "adding to the beauty of the past," 16, 145, 193n5; and the theatre, 3, 7, 9, 23, 39; Arts and Letters Club, 6, 188n19; as performer, 3, 5–6, 8, 15, 23, 192n49; Canada Council Medal, 14; choral music 1, 7, 11, 16, 20, 163; Church of St. Mary Magdalene, 7–8, 12–13, 15; Companion of the Order of Canada, 14; compositional fingerprints, 27, 29, 35, 48, 66, 84–85, 95, 102–3, 107–8, 112–13, 122, 125, 147, 162, 194n3; counterpoint, 2, 16, 20, 24, 26, 36, 42, 45, 58, 63, 88–89, 96–97, 106–8, 116, 118, 122, 127, 140, 154–55, 186–87n9;

"Dean of English Canadian composers," 1, 17; death, 15; early life, 2–3; "English by birth, Irish by extraction, Canadian by adoption and Scotch by absorption," 1, 186n5; English Church Union, 4, 25; fanfare, 11, 25, 28, 36–37, 48, 50–51, 96, 108, 131–33, 138, 151, 153–56, 169, 174–75, 206n30; fauxbourdon, 4, 11, 169–70, 187–88n15; Fellow of the Royal College of Organists, 3; Fellow of the Royal School of Music, 14; form, 48, 55–56, 66, 78, 81–82, 84, 86, 88–89, 95–96, 98, 100, 103, 105, 109–11, 113, 121–22, 126, 128, 131, 134, 136, 147, 158, 164–65, 200n10; fugue/fugato, 20, 27–28, 58–59, 63, 98, 111, 117, 119–20, 126–28, 130, 143, 146–48, 165–67, 205n18; Guild of All Souls, 4, 25; harmony, 24, 26–36, 40, 46, 48–49, 58, 63–64, 66–67, 69–70, 74, 78, 80, 83, 86–87, 89–90, 97, 100–01, 108–9, 111–12, 116, 119–21, 131, 136, 146–51, 154–56, 170–71, 174–77, 198n3, 200n8, 201n17; health, 11, 13–14, 66, 157; honorary degrees, 6, 13–14, 65; interest in numerology, 5–6; *klangfarbenmelodie*, 130; Lambeth Degree of Doctor of Music, 12; Lombard Rhythm (Scotch Snap), 36, 50, 195n11; "love music," 121, 125; *Man Of Music*, 13; melody, 20, 36, 38, 43–44, 48–49, 55, 60–61, 62–63, 66, 75–77, 81, 112, 118, 121–22, 133–34, 148, 155–57, 164; move to Toronto, 5; "mystical chorus," 34, 111, 187n12; National Award of Merit University of Alberta Banff School of Fine Arts, 12–13; orchestral music, xvii, 3, 7–8, 10, 20, 23, 38, 93, 181–82; orchestration, 20–21, 33–34, 36, 38, 40, 42–44, 51, 55, 62–63, 65, 67, 70, 74–76, 79–80, 82–83, 85, 90, 97–98, 100–03, 105, 107, 111–13, 117–18, 120, 123–27, 129, 133, 141, 158–61, 198n4, 198n7; organist University of Toronto, 8; organ music, 1, 7, 16; percussion, 35, 85, 94–95, 99, 138, 154, 161, 163–67, 176; phrasing, 27, 29–30, 41, 49–51, 66, 68, 70, 86–87, 141, 147, 155, 158–60, 165, 170–71; plainchant, 2, 25; "Tristan chord," 201n15; St. John the Baptist Kensington, 4, 6, 20; St. Paul's Bloor Street, 5–7, 11, 13–15; St. Saviour's Church choir school, 2; songs, 20; "sprung rhythm," 127, 136; "strange sounds, which surprise and disturb me," 16; stretto, 31–32, 59, 109, 136, 143, 148, 165, 167; Thalian Operatic Society, 4; transitions, 28, 44–45, 55, 5, 17, 63, 83–84, 97–98, 124–25, 133, 155–56; Tudor Singers, 4, 8; University Player's Club at Hart House, 7; Wanstead Choral Society, 3; "Willan motto," 81, 87, 90, 105, 107–9, 124–25, 129, 134–35; "Willan rush," 35, 37, 44–46, 66, 104, 119, 158, 195n8, 195n9; wind band music, xvii, 11, 17, 20, 138, 181–82

—WORKS: *[Allegro marcato]*, 24–25, 183; *All Hail! All Hail!*, 3, 20; *A Marching Tune*, 10, 21, 55–57, 152, 181; *An Apostrophe to the Heavenly Hosts*, 7, 12, 16; *A Prayer of Rejoicing*, 192n43; *Ave verum corpus*, 5, 58; *Ballade*, 73–77, 190n37; *Blessed Art Thou, O Lord*, 191n40; *Brébeuf and His Brethren*, 10, 15, 39, 58; *Celtic Sketches No. 1*, 62; *Centennial Anthem*, 14, 65, 157; *Centennial March (Ceremonial March)*, xvii, 14, 65–68, 85, 138, 181, 184, 210n1; *Ceremonial March for the Canadian Centennial*, 139, 157–62, 182, 184, 206n32; *Choral March*, 60; *Coronation March (Marche solennelle)*, 9, 47–54, 59–60, 62, 68, 85, 181, 195n7, 200n4; *Coronation Suite*, 12, 192n44; *Coronation Te Deum*, 9; *Cymbeline*, 60; *Darest Thou Now O Soul Walk Out with Me toward the Unknown Region*, 195n13; *Deirdre of the Sorrows*, 10, 15–17, 90; *Dreams*, 100; *Élégie héroïque*, 138–39, 152–57, 182, 184 ; *Elegy*, 69, 71; *Epilogue*, 25–29, 106, 181, 183, 198n16; *Fair in Face*, 7; *Fanfare*, 169–71, 182, 184, 208n1; *Farewell*, 193n1; *Fugue in G Minor*, 58–59, 184; *Gloria Deo per immense saecula*, 191n40; *Great is the Lord*, 191n40; *Healey Willan Song Album No. 2*, 196n8; *Hymn to the Sun*, 38; *I Beheld Her*, 7; *In the Name of God We Will Set Up Our Banners*, 6; Introduction